HAPPY & WHOLE

Magdalena Roze

HAPPY & WHOLE

*Wholefood recipes and ideas to
nourish the body, soul and home*

Photography by

Rob Palmer

plum. Pan Macmillan Australia

This book is for Mum and Dad, for instilling in me a love of food and showing me that family is everything.

CONTENTS

INTRODUCTION

This book is about the joy of cooking and sharing food, slowing down and moving towards a more natural and balanced way of nourishing ourselves. It's nothing new, and even a few decades ago this way of living would have been the norm, but in our busy, modern lives these holistic and traditional ways of living seem to have been forgotten. *Happy & Whole* is about enjoying wholefoods, wellness, nurturing your home, spending time outdoors and being creative. While I have always gravitated towards a more natural lifestyle, making a sea change to Byron Bay and embracing motherhood has deepened my connection with food and inspired me to learn more about nutritious, ethical produce and a lifestyle that's more nourishing for me and my family. I'm still learning after writing this book and the more I learn, the more I realise it's about keeping things as simple as possible (and importantly, not about being perfect!).

There are so many conflicting messages about what we should and shouldn't eat, which can lead to confusion and even take the enjoyment out of food. So for me, it's all about balance and a commonsense approach that focuses on real, unprocessed, nutrient-rich foods that make us feel good and are as close to their natural state as possible. That's it. It's not about trends, superfoods, diets or cutting anything out. In fact, I try to include as much deliciousness as possible, and that includes cakes, breads, pasta and wine. It's just that I don't have them all the time. This is what makes my approach to food sustainable and enjoyable. I've written this book because I want to share my favourite wholefood recipes, rituals and go-to tips from beauty to nourishing your home that bring me happiness and comfort, in the hope that they will enrich your life in some way, too.

Of course, being a meteorologist, this book is also about the weather. I can't help but see life (especially what I eat) through a weather lens. Food and weather are two universal things that connect us all, no matter who you are. They tickle our senses and affect our moods and decisions. Whether we realise it or not, what we feel like eating is greatly inspired by the weather, and the chapters in this book reflect this. Sunny is all about salads, picnics and refreshing drinks; Humid celebrates cooling dishes, such as popsicles, seafood and tropical, Asian flavours; overcast days have us longing for warming dishes, so Cloudy features soups, pastas and stews; and, finally, Rainy is about rejuvenation and restoration, with recipes for baking, preserving and slow-cooking.

MY FOOD FOUNDATIONS

My life has always pretty much revolved around food and family. I've been making a mess in the kitchen since I was about seven years old. I grew up in an Eastern European household where wholesome meals made from scratch were the norm, soups and broths were an obligatory starter to every meal, and fermented ingredients, such as funky krauts and gherkins regularly made it into the school lunchbox, sadly at a time when they were seriously uncool. Sweets made an appearance during celebrations, but we weren't exactly deprived as my parents would always find something to celebrate! They'd bust out the vodka, cheese and Polish doughnuts if the neighbour so much as got a new washing machine! We knew nothing about gut health then, it was just the way Mum cooked because it was cheap, and that's how she used to get through the freezing winters in Russia and Poland. Never mind that it was boiling hot in the Australian burbs! But, looking back, it's these things that have shaped my cooking and love of wholefoods. And, it's probably no surprise that I ended up with a chef (in fact, we first met while cooking together on a food show, but that's another story!). Making the sea change to Byron Bay has evolved my passion for good food even further, by connecting me to local producers and the many inspiring ideas around food and how to get the most out of what we eat.

HOW MY SEA CHANGE CHANGED ME

If you had asked me a few years ago what I'd be doing today, I never would have imagined I'd be a mother, living in Byron Bay and writing my first cookbook! It's the furthest thing from where I was at in my busy television career in Sydney. But, when my partner Darren got the opportunity to open a restaurant on a farm (a chef's dream!), the offer was too good to miss and without hesitation I said, "Let's do it!" In retrospect, I'm actually surprised that I didn't give more thought or consideration to the impact this would have on my television career and social life. A few months later, we were literally living the dream in Byron Bay, but I'd be filtering this story if I didn't admit that I felt a bit lost and lonely. All I had ever known was working in the media, working crazy, long hours, attending lots of social events and burning the candle at both ends. My foot was always on the accelerator. I'd never actually slowed down and at first it felt quite foreign. *What was I going to do?* Three months later I fell pregnant, and knowing that I wasn't going to chase my old life for a while, I decided to just let go, surrender and use the opportunity to do what I love. So, I cooked, and baked, and burnt things. I pickled. I visited farms and asked questions. Then, I cooked some more. I returned to my Eastern European roots and the old, simple ways of preparing wholefoods like my mother and grandmother, and I never felt better or more nourished. This was especially important, as I was feeding not only me but my baby, too. I had never seen food that looked and tasted so good, and I knew I couldn't go back. I also realised that being close to a food's source made healthy eating so much easier and I wanted to share this with others. So, I started

writing about it on my blog and discovered that other people were looking for a taste of that sea change life, too. And here we are.

KEEPING IT REAL

It's very easy to fall into the 'Byron bubble'. Anyone who's been here knows that it's a pretty special place. There's a reason why so many people from around the world gravitate here. Maybe it's the alternative lifestyle and therapies, tight-knit community, or perhaps it's the exceptional food, rainforests and beaches. Some say it's the huge obsidian black crystal beneath the earth! Whatever it is, it's magnetic. I grew up in the city, yet I've grown so accustomed to the slower pace of life that I now find the local town of Mullumbimby hectic when I can't find a park! But, I go back to the big smoke often enough to be reminded that living in a place with such fertile land, passionate farmers and amazing produce makes it a lot easier to live a simpler, more natural life. I still love the city – the culture, restaurants and energy – but with that comes less time, more traffic and greater work pressures. I can't help but laugh at myself that in such a hectic environment the idea of soaking grains or making things from scratch, such as your own nut milk, seem far more complicated than buying something ready-made at the supermarket. Maybe a more appropriate title would have been *How to Complicate Your Life?!* But that doesn't mean it's impossible. It comes down to balance and doing the best you can under the circumstances. Something like soaking grains is actually super easy, it's just a matter of habit, and even one fresh meal a day is something to enjoy and celebrate, so don't beat yourself up or feel guilty if you don't achieve everything you want.

I've also written this book because I love sharing what I've learned from living in Byron Bay about food, wellness and motherhood. When I first gave birth to Archie I remember being so bewildered and filled with questions. I was thirsty for any tips and stories from other mums about how they do things, even if I didn't necessarily adopt all of them. I've been lucky enough to meet some amazing people here from doctors, acupuncturists and lactation experts to chefs, wellness advocates and other mums, so if there's anything I can pass on to help another person, spark a conversation or provide a bit of inspiration, then great!

MY FOOD NON-PHILOSOPHY

My philosophy is that I don't really have one! There are so many different diets and lifestyles all claiming to be the 'best' or the 'healthiest', that it can be very difficult working out what to eat. To simplify things and put the power back in your own hands, I find it helpful to try and get back-to-basics. By this, I mean eating wholefoods that are unprocessed, grown without the use of sprays and chemicals and are as close to their natural source as possible. However, this also needs to include foods that *work for you*. I don't necessarily believe that any one ingredient is more special or nutritious than another. Rather, its nutritional worth comes down to *how* it's grown and prepared. A lovingly grown spray-free carrot is just as good as more on-trend foods, such as kale.

I also don't see any particular food as 'good' or 'bad'. Sure, cakes and marshmallows aren't as nutrient-rich as a bowl of chicken broth, but they are 'sometimes' foods and, for me, perfectly fine on occcasion, especially if they're made with real, whole ingredients. Sometimes, a lovely piece of cake and a

cup of tea is the only thing that hits the spot on a rainy afternoon. When I do cook with sweeteners, I generally use unrefined options such as honey, maple syrup, palm, coconut or rapadura sugars, as they're more mineral-rich than processed sugars. In this book, you will find a couple of recipes where caster sugar makes a cameo, but that's because the other sugars don't provide the same delicious result! If you're going to bake a cake, you must enjoy it!

Many of the recipes in this book are also dairy and gluten free along with plenty of vegan and vegetarian options because that's how I like to eat. While I enjoy dairy, most of the time almond milk is my preferred option as I love the nutty taste. I also generally choose wholegrains, such as spelt and quinoa over wheat flour (unless it's a baguette!).

THE WHOLE PICTURE

Being happy, whole and fulfilled isn't just about food. I believe that all aspects of life need to be fed and nurtured including relationships, the home, lifestyle habits, your mind and what you put on your skin. Bringing nature into the home with flowers and plants, and simply being creative and making things by hand are nourishing and good for the soul. It's a lovely way to add a bespoke nature to special occasions and gifts for people. I loved making the decorations for my baby shower farm picnic and one of my favourite accessories is a homemade flower crown which I've shared on page 146.

It's challenging to live a completely chemical-free life in our modern world, but there are huge benefits to becoming more conscious about the ingredients in our skin-care and household products. You'd be surprised how many toxins are completely unnecessary and easily replaceable with natural options that are so much safer and effective.

After years of putting heavy make-up on my face for television, my skin broke out in rashes and nothing worked until I overhauled my skin-care routine and began making my own 100 per cent natural creams. My skin improved in a day. I still wear make-up, but it's amazing how after a couple of years of using natural skin-care products, I find the smells of conventional creams, sprays and perfumes unbearable and quite toxic. Try some of my natural skin-care recipes on page 189 and see for yourself.

MY TIPS FOR CREATING NOURISHING MEALS

Take baby steps

Don't feel like you need to overhaul your entire pantry or life in a quest to be healthier, as it's just not sustainable. Set yourself a little goal of doing something new each week, such as getting in the habit of soaking your grains before cooking them. It literally takes seconds to do and cuts minutes off the cooking time the next day. The only chore is remembering, something I often fail to do, mind you!

Stock the pantry

Good-quality canned food, such as beans and jars of pasta sauce, made with organic, natural ingredients make whipping up a delicious meal quick and easy on the busy days.

Buy in bulk

I barely have any time to shop with a baby, so I like to stock up on all my whole flours, nuts, seeds, powders and oils in one go. It's cheaper this way and enables you to create simple dishes on a whim.

Experiment

Use the rainy days to get your cook on – learn, stuff-up and triumph! Trust me, it's very empowering and you'll start *wanting* to cook more.

Make the farmers' market a ritual

Get to know your local farmers' market. Nothing beats locally grown, spray-free, just-picked fruit and vegetables, plus the diversity of produce is amazing.

Back yourself

I will never forget the first time I cooked a meal for Darren, a *chef*! I was so nervous, the pots and pans were dropping everywhere. Since then, he's given me the confidence to cook the dishes I know, to make mistakes and embrace the meals that don't work out. He once said to me that it's the off-cuts, the burnt bits, the overhanging crust and the wonky things that chefs really love. Embrace the imperfection!

A FEW NOTES ON INGREDIENTS

When I refer to any meat, eggs or dairy, I try and seek out free-range, pasture-fed produce wherever possible for nutrition and ethical reasons. Happy animals that are allowed to roam in their natural environment without stress will always be more wholesome and tasty.

Dairy is full cream

Fat is essential for digesting the protein in milk. I particularly like cultured dairy, such as yoghurt, butter, créme fraîche and buttermilk. They're not only delicious but the good bacteria in these foods is great for the gut.

Favourite cooking fats

My go-to cooking fats are ghee and coconut oil for their high smoke point and flavour.

Get funky

I always have fermented foods such as sauerkraut in the fridge. They're one of the best ways to dose up any meal with vitamins when there's 'nothing to eat'.

The saviours

Fresh eggs and frozen peas make a great base for a last-minute meal, and frozen bananas and berries make it very easy to whip up a quick smoothie. But, if I had to choose one secret weapon it would be pesto. Pesto makes everything taste better from the humble avo' on toast to pasta or an omelette.

If you've actually continued to read up until this point, I'm blown away that you took the time to do so! I hope this book provides you a little magic, a fulfilling meal or even a nugget of gold that sparks a conversation or journey that helps you. Perhaps it might inspire you to slow down, simplify things and create small 'moments' each day that add to that feeling of wholeness. This book is not about achieving perfection, in fact, I don't even think that's possible. Just as the weather is in constant movement and flux, so are we, moving towards balance but never quite attaining it. Nature flourishes in this dynamic and we, too, should embrace the highs and lows and accept them as part of the natural flow of life. It's a necessary part of being happy and whole.

Happy cooking x x x

SUNRISE

NOURISHING RECIPES FOR BREAKFAST.
OATS, EGGS, SMOOTHIES, BOWLS OF GOODNESS.

Sunrise is that magical part of the day when anything seems possible. You've just had a great night's sleep, and you rise to the first light feeling refreshed. While the morning fog lifts, yoga, surfing or a run on the beach clears the mind. It's the smell of dew on the grass and fresh warm eggs from the chook pen. Other days it's sleeping in, cozy and warm under a cloud of blankets not knowing or caring what the time is. Sometimes, the frost on the grass allows for more warm cuddles and breakfast in bed. It's the smell of coffee, the sound of the kettle boiling water for peppermint tea, the Sunday papers. It's warm rays on the kitchen table, the first thirst-quenching glass of water and freshly squeezed juice sipped on the deck, while your senses awaken and you stretch. The sunrise inspires new beginnings and fresh intentions. Your nourishing energy sets you up for the day. Good morning.

BUCKWHEAT PANCAKES WITH HAZELNUTS, STRAWBERRIES AND BASIL

MAKES 10–12 PANCAKES

These wholesome and filling pancakes are a regular Sunday breakfast in our house. I use buckwheat flour because I love the rich, nutty flavour, so the fact that it's incredibly nutritious is a bonus! Contrary to its name, buckwheat is neither related to wheat nor is it a grain. It's the seed of a plant from the rhubarb family, so it's gluten free and easily digestible. It's also high in protein, antioxidants, magnesium, trace minerals such as manganese, and may contribute to reducing blood sugar levels after meals. Yup, these pancakes are good for you. If you have leftovers, they keep well in the fridge for a couple of days. The trick to ensuring perfect, fluffy pancakes is to add the whisked egg whites to the batter just before you're ready to fry. If you're entertaining friends for brunch, you can make the batter the night before and refrigerate it. Just add the whisked egg whites to the batter in the morning – quick and easy!

70 g (½ cup) hazelnuts
3 eggs, separated
60 g butter, melted
500 ml (2 cups) buttermilk
    or whey (for a recipe see
    page 86)
300 g (2 cups) buckwheat flour
1 teaspoon bicarbonate of soda
pinch of sea salt
ghee or coconut oil, for frying

To serve

maple syrup or raw honey
sheep's milk yoghurt
strawberries, hulled and
    quartered
small basil leaves

Preheat the oven to 180°C and line a baking tray with baking paper.

Sprinkle the hazelnuts on the prepared tray and roast for 10–15 minutes.

In a large bowl, whisk together the egg yolks, melted butter and buttermilk or whey. Add the flour, bicarb soda and salt and mix well.

Whisk the egg whites in a separate bowl until they form soft peaks. Gently fold the egg whites into the batter just before you're ready to cook.

Place a large frying pan over medium heat and grease with a little ghee or coconut oil. When the pan is hot, ladle in the batter to form pancakes 10–12 cm in diameter. Once bubbles start forming (about 2 minutes), flip the pancakes. Don't worry about making perfectly identical shapes. I reckon a stack of fluffy golden pancakes looks better when they're beautifully uneven! Transfer the cooked pancakes to a plate and cover with a clean tea towel, so they stay warm while you cook the remaining batter.

When the hazelnuts are golden and aromatic, remove them from the oven and wrap in a clean tea towel to steam for 1 minute. Rub the hazelnuts in the tea towel to remove the skins, then roughly chop.

To serve, stack two or three pancakes on a plate with a drizzle of maple syrup or honey between each one. Serve with a generous dollop of sheep's milk yoghurt, a small handful of strawberries, a sprinkle of basil leaves and the hazelnuts.

CARROT CAKE PORRIDGE

SERVES 3-4

This recipe is inspired by a dish I had at Grød in Copenhagen – a cafe completely devoted to porridge! Darren and I went there for breakfast every morning during our week-long holiday, and this tiny place was always packed with Danish foodies and their kids tucking into all sorts of amazing porridges, such as oats with apple compote and caramel sauce or lunch versions such as dhal and congee. This recipe is the perfect balance between sweet/savoury and creamy/crunchy thanks to the mixed grains and toasted nuts. But there's more to love about this bowl of goodness than just the texture and taste. You're getting good fats from the almonds and coconut oil, vitamin A from the carrots, antioxidants from the spices and protein from the grains. To get the most nutritional value from your grains (and to make them more digestible), soak them overnight in a bowl of water with a squeeze of lemon juice or apple cider vinegar at room temperature. To make this nice and easy, I've selected grains that have a similar cooking time. I hope you'll love it as much as we do.

65 g (⅓ cup) millet

65 g (⅓ cup) quinoa

30 g (⅓ cup) rolled oats

2 teaspoons vanilla extract
  or powder

1 teaspoon ground cinnamon

1 teaspoon grated ginger

½ teaspoon ground nutmeg

40 g (¼ cup) chopped almonds

20 g (¼ cup) shredded coconut

1 carrot, grated

125 ml (½ cup) almond milk
  (for a recipe see page 47)

1 tablespoon maple syrup
  (see note)

1 tablespoon coconut oil

Place the millet, quinoa, oats, vanilla, cinnamon, ginger and nutmeg in a saucepan with 625 ml (2½ cups) of water (or 500 ml/2 cups if the grains have been soaked). Bring to a simmer over medium heat, partially cover with a lid and cook for about 20 minutes, or until the liquid has been absorbed.

Meanwhile, toast the almonds and shredded coconut in a small frying pan over medium heat, stirring frequently, for 3–4 minutes until golden and fragrant. Remove from the heat and set aside.

When most of the porridge liquid has been absorbed, stir in the grated carrot and almond milk. Remove from the heat, cover and let it rest for about 5 minutes. Just before serving, stir in the maple syrup and coconut oil and top with the toasted almonds and coconut.

NOTES

• If you have a juicer, you can replace one of the cups of water with fresh carrot juice to give the porridge an even more amazing flavour.

• You can use raw honey in place of the maple syrup if you like.

BREAKFAST PROTEIN COOKIES

MAKES 10–12

These are no ordinary cookies! The oats, buckwheat flour and coconut provide energy, while the nuts and seeds not only add a delicious texture but also lots of protein, fibre and good fats. In addition, the 'hidden' white beans provide extra protein and ensure that you feel nice and full. These cookies are naturally a bit crumbly, so storing them in the fridge helps the ingredients bind. They're the perfect thing to make on a weekend and have on standby for a delicious and wholesome breakfast. Get some fresh air and enjoy them on a morning walk!

180 g (2 cups) oats

110 g (1 cup) buckwheat flour

40 g (½ cup) shredded coconut

1 teaspoon baking powder

1 teaspoon bicarbonate of soda

1 teaspoon ground cinnamon

½ teaspoon ground nutmeg

½ teaspoon sea salt

1 x 400 g can white cannellini
    beans, drained and rinsed

60 ml (¼ cup) melted coconut oil

80 ml (⅓ cup) maple syrup

1 egg

2 teaspoons vanilla extract
    or powder

zest of ½ orange

1 cup mixed nuts and seeds
    (e.g. pumpkin seeds, sunflower
    seeds, chopped hazelnuts)

70 g (½ cup) raisins or
    chopped dates

Preheat the oven to 180°C and line a large baking tray with baking paper.

Place 1 cup of the oats in a food processor and blitz to a coarse crumb. Transfer the ground oats to a large bowl along with the remaining oats, buckwheat flour, shredded coconut, baking powder, bicarb soda, cinnamon, nutmeg and salt and mix well.

Place the beans, coconut oil, maple syrup and egg in a food processor and blitz until creamy. Add the vanilla and orange zest and pulse to combine.

Add the wet bean mixture to the dry ingredients and mix well with a spoon or by hand. Fold in the nuts, seeds and raisins or dates.

Roll heaped tablespoonfuls of the mixture into balls and place them on the prepared tray, pressing them with a spatula to flatten, and spacing them about 2 cm apart. If your dough is quite sticky, flour your hands to make shaping the cookies easier.

Bake for 20 minutes or until golden brown. Cool on a wire rack for 10 minutes then transfer to the fridge for 1 hour to set a little more – if you can wait!

These cookies will keep for up to 7 days in a sealed container in the fridge. You can also freeze them for up to 1 month.

MISO-MAPLE COCONUT OATS

SERVES 2 (AND A LITTLE EXTRA FOR SECONDS)

Miso in porridge? Absolutely! The salty miso and sweet maple syrup give this porridge a delicious salted caramel flavour. Add to this the crunch of pecans and creaminess of coconut milk and you have a heavenly combination! But apart from the 'umami' flavour (the mysterious 'fifth taste') that miso adds to a dish, there are other reasons why the Japanese have been starting their day with a bowl of this delicious ingredient for thousands of years. Miso, which is fermented soybean, is rich in enzymes and probiotics, high in complete proteins and very high in vitamins and minerals, making it beneficial for our digestive, immune and cardiovascular systems. It's the perfect way to start the day.

90 g (1 cup) oats

250 ml (1 cup) coconut milk, plus extra (optional)

1 heaped tablespoon white miso paste

1 tablespoon maple syrup, plus extra for drizzling

1 apple, skin on, cored and grated

30 g (¼ cup) pecans, chopped

1 tablespoon shredded coconut

Place the oats, coconut milk and 250 ml (1 cup) of water in a saucepan over medium heat. Bring to the boil, then reduce the heat and simmer for 4–5 minutes, stirring occasionally. After a minute or so, stir in the miso and maple syrup. Continue to simmer over low heat, stirring often, until the liquid has been absorbed. To make it nice and creamy, you can add an extra ¼ cup of water or coconut milk and simmer for a further 1 minute.

Remove the porridge from the heat, cover and allow it to sit for a couple of minutes. Give it another stir and taste, adding a little more miso or maple syrup, if desired.

To serve, divide between bowls and top with the grated apple, chopped pecans, shredded coconut and a little drizzle of maple syrup. You can reheat any leftovers on the stove with a little water or coconut milk.

SUNDAY MORNING WAFFLES

SERVES 3–4

Ah waffles... one of the dreamiest aromas that can float out of any kitchen on a Sunday morning! Even though this recipe contains maple syrup, these waffles actually work just as well with savoury toppings. If it's sunny, I like to keep the flavours fresh with yoghurt, fruit and seeds. While on a cool or cloudy day, avocado, chopped tomatoes, sour cream and a poached egg hit the spot. These waffles are a treat, and by that I mean that they're full of wonderful, wholefood ingredients, including spelt, linseeds, eggs and yoghurt that are nutritious yet won't leave you feeling bloated. And don't limit these waffles to breakfast – they make a great lunch and dinner, too! To make life a little easier, you can prepare the batter the night before.

2 tablespoons linseeds

100 ml warm water

260 g unbleached spelt flour (see note)

2 teaspoons baking powder

½ teaspoon cinnamon

½ teaspoon sea salt

1 egg

310 ml (1¼ cups) milk (any kind!)

140 g (½ cup) Greek yoghurt

2 tablespoons maple syrup

2 tablespoons coconut oil, melted and slightly cooled

1 teaspoon vanilla extract

ghee or coconut oil, for greasing

To serve

melted ghee or coconut oil

Greek yoghurt

mixed fresh berries

toasted flaked almonds

maple syrup

Preheat a waffle iron.

Place the linseeds and warm water in a small bowl and set aside to soak and form a gel while you prepare the other ingredients.

Sift the flour, baking powder, cinnamon and salt into a bowl. Tip in any bran left behind in the sifter and mix thoroughly.

In another bowl, whisk the egg then add the milk, yoghurt, maple syrup, coconut oil and vanilla and whisk again until combined. Mix in the linseed gel. Add the wet ingredients to the dry ingredients and mix with a spatula or wooden spoon until just combined.

When the waffle iron is heated, grease the wells with a little ghee or coconut oil, then ladle in up to ½ cup of the batter and close. Cook for about 6–8 minutes or until golden brown and crisp. Remove from the iron and transfer to a plate. Repeat with the remaining batter.

To serve, brush the waffles with a little melted ghee or coconut oil, top with a generous dollop of yoghurt, sprinkle with berries and flaked almonds and drizzle with maple syrup. Eat in bed!

NOTE

If you use wholemeal spelt flour, add a little more milk to the batter as it absorbs more liquid.

MOTHER–BABY NOURISHMENT

I've always been deeply connected with food and its role in
our health and wellbeing, and when I fell pregnant I became
a lot more conscious about eating foods that were not
only beneficial for the baby's growth and development
but also my own wellness.

I must preface this by saying that I'm not an expert in this area, and there's enough judgement around parenting as it is. My journey is one of many different approaches to choose from. I'm just keen to share what I've learned on the chance there are others out there who are asking similar questions.

Once I started to do some research, I quickly became overwhelmed by the minefield of conflicting information about what I should eat. It got to the point where it seemed easier to eat a bag of chips than risk a salad or sandwich from a cafe! So I sifted through the information (and the science that backed it up) and came up with a range of wholefoods to eat throughout my pregnancy that worked beautifully for both me and my baby.

Eggs

I ate two a day – they contain all nine of the essential protein-building amino acids, a stack of vitamins (all the B vitamins, plus A, D, E and K) as well as minerals including iron, phosphorus and potassium. The quality of the eggs, however, is also important. I ate organic eggs from local pasture-raised chickens, which are super nutritious, and I made sure they were well cooked. If you can't source pasture-raised eggs, try to choose free range and organic (see page 54 for more on eggs).

Oranges

These were my biggest craving. At one stage, I was having three or four a day! Interestingly, I found out that I was low in iron, and vitamin C is a key nutrient in iron absorption – I love how my body was telling me what I needed.

Beef

With all the extra iron required for the creation of the placenta, I increased my intake of pasture-raised beef to at least twice a week.

Bone broth

I can't speak highly enough about bone broth and its incredible healing qualities. It's packed with minerals (including calcium, magnesium, phosphorus, silicon and sulphur), gelatine and glycosaminoglycans such as keratin and hyaluronic acid, which are all amazing for skin, teeth, bones,

hair and nails. I was drinking about a cup a day during winter as a snack, but you can make a meal out of it by adding grains, meat and veggies. Check out my Healing Chicken Broth recipe on page 212.

Full-cream dairy

I'm all for full-cream dairy – there's a good reason for the fat being there: it's essential for digesting the protein in the milk. Plus it tastes so good! It also contains all nine essential amino acids, along with minerals and vitamins. I enjoyed organic milk, hard cheese and yoghurt throughout my pregnancy.

Fish

Oily fish, such as salmon, sardines, tuna, mackerel and snapper contain high amounts of long-chain omega 3 fatty acids. These are essential fatty acids (meaning we have to get them from our diet) and are important for brain and nervous system function. Unfortunately, I did not feel like eating fish while pregnant, so I took omega 3 supplements.

Fruit and vegetables

Most of what I ate was organic and free of chemical sprays as I either bought them from local producers or at farmers' markets.

What about the sweet stuff?

I avoided refined sugar and processed foods for most of my pregnancy, especially the first two trimesters and, fortunately, I didn't really crave them. By the third trimester I often craved pastry and ice cream, so I enjoyed them now and again.

What I avoided

While I love oysters, prawns, sushi, beef carpaccio and creamy brie, I abstained from raw meat and fish, shellfish and soft, mould-ripened cheeses, as per the official recommendations. There's nothing wrong with these foods, it's just that there's a slight chance of contamination with listeria bacteria which can affect the baby, so it's a risk I didn't want to take. My goodness it was incredible to have a little camembert and some oysters after the baby was born!

POST-PREGNANCY AND BREASTFEEDING

The importance of wholefoods in my diet became even greater post-pregnancy for healing and boosting milk supply. After building life during pregnancy, giving birth and then nourishing the baby 24 hours a day, it's no surprise that a lot of mothers become exhausted. This is more than just being 'tired', it's actually postnatal depletion and is a real condition.

In some countries and cultures, such as China, there is a tradition of 'confinement' where new mothers stay at home and take care of themselves for at least 30 days, while 'confinement women' cook them nourishing foods, do the cleaning and help look after the baby to give the mother the opportunity to heal. How good would that be!

I'm sure you've heard the expression, 'it takes a village to raise a child', yet many parents are doing it solo, often without the support of extended family let alone the broader community, and have little time or energy to restore themselves. While I enjoyed a wonderful pregnancy, I didn't 'bounce back' very well afterwards and had ongoing issues with my breastmilk supply. I was so depleted after labour that I had no milk for a week and had to work very hard to build and maintain my supply throughout the whole breastfeeding journey. It took a few months to establish and then seemed to reach a comfortable point for both of us. I was conscientious about pumping breastmilk to help stimulate supply, and I ate milk-boosting foods such as egg yolks and bone broths, as well as having regular acupuncture treatment and taking fenugreek (in tablet form). While there is limited scientific evidence for the efficacy of fenugreek as a galactagogue (the promotion of lactation), some preliminary studies have shown encouraging results.

I'm not going to lie, it was exhausting at times. It's hard to pinpoint what ultimately helped me, but I was willing to try everything – it was so important for me to breastfeed Archie for the comfort and closeness, as well as to give him the nutrients and antibodies he needed. There were times when I felt broken and wondered how long I'd be able to continue, but when I was able to nourish him on breastmilk alone through a bout of baby gastro, get him to sleep through teething and soothe him on hectic airplane journeys, I knew it was worth the effort!

I know this isn't the path for everyone, as breastfeeding can be very difficult or impossible for some women. This was the journey that felt right for me, but every mother knows what's best for herself and her baby.

EMOTIONAL NOURISHMENT

Motherhood is challenging at times (it definitely has been for me), so it's important to gather a tribe of supportive people around us. I honestly wouldn't have gotten through a lot of tough times without the help of some incredibly wise women and men, and I continue to rely on a network of friends, family and experts to guide me. The other important thing I'd recommend is a sense of humour!

YIN 'N' YANG GREEN SMASH ON RYE

SERVES 4

I could have left it at peas, feta, mint and lemon, but I couldn't resist adding the avocado and rye bread, making this the ultimate savoury breakfast – packed with nutrients to keep you going all day. While fresh peas are always preferable, the humble frozen pea holds its own when it comes to nutrients, fibre and, of course, convenience, so I've always got a bag in the freezer. And here's a little factoid on peas: while they're a great source of protein, they don't have the complete package of amino acids – being high in lysine (great for building bones and antibodies) but lacking methionine (important in nerve function and liver repair). Wholegrains like rye, on the other hand, have the opposite composition, so they make the perfect yang to the peas' yin!

400 g (3⅓ cups) fresh or
    frozen peas
2 spring onions, thinly sliced
2 tablespoons crème fraîche
    or Greek yoghurt
2 tablespoons shredded mint,
    plus extra small leaves to serve
juice of ½ lemon, plus lemon
    wedges to serve
sea salt and freshly ground
    black pepper
2 tablespoons extra-virgin
    olive oil
4 thick slices of sourdough
    rye bread
1 avocado, thickly sliced
100 g marinated Persian feta,
    crumbled (see note)
2 handfuls of watercress
1 pear, cored and thinly sliced
2 tablespoons roughly chopped
    toasted walnuts
1 tablespoon toasted pumpkin
    seeds
1 tablespoon toasted sunflower
    seeds
pinch of chilli flakes

Put your favourite tunes on.

Cook the peas in boiling salted water for 4–5 minutes, then drain. Using a potato masher, coarsely crush the peas until softened but still a little chunky. Add the spring onion, crème fraîche or yoghurt, mint and 1 teaspoon of the lemon juice. Season to taste, cover and set aside.

Meanwhile, heat a chargrill pan over medium–high heat. Drizzle half of the oil over the bread slices and cook on both sides until golden and toasted. Top the toast with the pea mixture, avocado and feta. Arrange the watercress, pear and walnuts in a small bowl.

Whisk the remaining lemon juice and oil in a small bowl and drizzle over everything. Scatter over the toasted seeds, chilli flakes and extra mint. Season with salt and pepper and serve with lemon wedges on the side.

NOTE

Persian feta is a marinated cow's milk feta made here in Australia. It's milder than Greek or Bulgarian feta, which is always made from sheep's and/or goat's milk. I like the Persian feta as it's smooth and packed with flavour, but feel free to use any feta you like!

CHICKEN AND GINGER CONGEE

SERVES 2 HUNGRY PEOPLE

Warming, medicinal and grounding, congee (rice porridge) is a nourishing way to start the day, especially when it's cold. This chicken and ginger version is from our friends Sarah and Jeremy from one of my favourite cafes, 100 Mile Table. I'm so chuffed they've shared this recipe with me. They were among the first friends we made when we moved to Byron, and I'm so grateful for their friendship, support and good food! And when I'm not in Byron, I still get to experience their warmth and hospitality by making my own bowl of this beautiful rice porridge. It's not enough to steal me away from their cafe, though – their bacon and egg butty and coffee has me hooked for good. The simple things are often the best.

1 cup cooked jasmine rice
200 g chicken thigh fillet,
    fat trimmed, diced
5 cm piece of ginger cut into
    matchsticks
good slug of Shaoxing wine
    (Chinese cooking wine)
good slug of light soy sauce
1 teaspoon sesame oil

To serve
finely shredded spring onions
fried shallots
freshly ground white pepper
chilli sauce

Place the cooked rice in a saucepan and cover with cold water by about 2 cm. Place over medium heat and bring to a simmer. Add the diced chicken and ginger along with the Shaoxing wine, soy and sesame oil. Stir well and simmer, partially covered, for 4–5 minutes or until the chicken is cooked through.

Taste the congee to make sure you have the right balance between the ginger, soy and Shaoxing (all soy sauces taste a little different and have different levels of salt, so you may need to add a little more). The consistency should be almost soupy.

Serve the congee topped with shredded spring onion, fried shallots, a pinch of white pepper and your favourite chilli sauce on the side. I occasionally like to serve a soft fried egg on top of the congee.

MEXICAN OMELETTE

SERVES 4

I love Mexican food. Avo, salsa, beans, corn, chilli. Oh my! Poor old black beans are so underrated in our neck of the woods that they rarely make an appearance on menus, but I'm trying to change that with this delicious omelette! This is the breakfast to make when you want something filling and spicy, and it's just as good for dinner. I've used canned beans in this recipe for convenience, but the best way to cook black beans is to soak dried ones overnight and cook them up a day before you need them – they're tastier and much more digestible.

8 eggs

2 tablespoons finely chopped
    chives

40 g salted butter

80 g manchego or vintage
    cheddar, grated

70 g snow pea sprouts or tendrils,
    for garnish

coriander leaves, for garnish

lime wedges, to serve

Salsa

1 corn cob, silk and husk removed

1 large tomato, deseeded and
    finely diced

1 avocado, diced

½ red onion, finely diced

1 fresh jalapeño chilli, deseeded
    and finely diced

3 coriander sprigs, leaves
    finely chopped

1 tablespoon avocado oil

juice of 1 lime

sea salt and freshly ground
    black pepper

Bean filling

1 tablespoon olive oil

1 onion, finely diced

1 garlic clove, crushed

¼ teaspoon ground cumin

¼ teaspoon ground coriander

2 truss tomatoes, finely chopped

1 tablespoon adobo sauce
    (see note)

160 g (1 cup) canned black beans,
    drained and rinsed

To make the salsa, place the corn on a chargrill pan over high heat for 8–10 minutes, turning frequently until cooked and charred all over. Set aside for 10 minutes to cool then carefully slice the kernels from the cob and transfer to a bowl. Add the tomato, avocado, onion, chilli, coriander leaves, oil and lime juice. Mix well and season to taste, then cover and refrigerate until needed.

To prepare the bean filling, heat the oil in a small saucepan over medium–high heat. Add the onion and cook for 2–3 minutes, stirring frequently, until softened. Add the garlic, cumin and coriander and cook for a further minute, stirring, until fragrant. Reduce the heat to low, add the tomato, adobo sauce and 60 ml (¼ cup) of water. Partially cover with a lid and cook, stirring occasionally, for 6–8 minutes until reduced by a third and thickened. Stir in the beans and cook until heated through, then season to taste. Transfer to a bowl and set aside until needed.

Lightly whisk the eggs in a bowl. Add the chives and a splash of water, then season. Heat a 20 cm non-stick frying pan over medium–high heat. Melt a quarter of the butter in the pan and add a quarter of the egg mixture, swirling to cover the base of the pan. Reduce the heat to medium. Scatter a quarter of the bean filling over one side of the omelette and top with a sprinkling of cheese. Cook for 1–2 minutes or until the egg is just starting to set. Fold the unfilled side of the omelette over to enclose the filling. Cook a further minute or so and carefully lift onto a serving plate. Repeat with the remaining ingredients.

Top the omelettes with the salsa and garnish with snow pea sprouts or tendrils and coriander leaves. Serve with lime wedges for squeezing over.

NOTES

- Adobo is a rich, smoky sauce made with chipotle chillies (smoke-dried jalapeños). If you can't find adobo sauce, replace it with 2 teaspoons of Tabasco or chilli powder.

- Double the delicious bean filling and you can use it for another meal – it stores well in the fridge for 2–3 days.

- Store leftover salsa in an airtight container for up to 2 days in the refrigerator. Toss through a salad or serve with chargrilled chicken for a go-to meal.

BIRDS' NESTS

SERVES 2

This breakfast is one of my staples because it has all the goodness I need to set me up for the day.
I had massive cravings for eggs when I was pregnant, which is not surprising as eggs are one of the most
complete foods you can eat. They are the hero of this dish, so you can treat the 'nest' like a blank canvas
for whatever you have in the fridge. If there's leftover rice or quinoa from dinner, or you happen to have
something pickled, such as kraut, add it in. This is best enjoyed with the Sunday papers or a crossword,
as Daz and I do. I know – very rock 'n' roll!

1 teaspoon olive oil

1 garlic clove, crushed

100 g kale and spinach leaves,
    roughly chopped
    (about 2 cups)

2 tablespoons mixed nuts
    and seeds (e.g. chopped
    almonds, sunflower seeds,
    pumpkin seeds)

3 tablespoons vinegar

2–4 eggs

1 avocado, sliced

handful of sprouts (e.g. sunflower,
    mung bean, alfalfa)

2 tablespoons chopped flat-leaf
    parsley leaves

pinch of chilli flakes (optional)

sea salt and freshly ground
    black pepper

Heat the olive oil in a small frying pan over medium heat and fry the
garlic for 1 minute until fragrant. Add the kale and spinach and cook for
1–2 minutes or until soft and wilted. Remove from the pan and set aside.
Using the same pan, toast your nuts and seeds for about 2 minutes or until
golden and fragrant, tossing them frequently so they don't burn. Set aside.

To poach the eggs, heat the vinegar and 1.5 litres (6 cups) of water in
a saucepan over medium heat until the water is trembling, then turn
the heat down so it stays at a gentle simmer. Gently crack the eggs into
the pan and cook for 3–4 minutes (don't touch them while they're cooking).
Remove the eggs with a slotted spoon and transfer to a small bowl.

To make the birds' nests, arrange the wilted greens, avocado and sprouts in
two shallow bowls in the shape of little nests. Carefully place the poached
egg (or eggs) in the centre. Garnish with the parsley, toasted nuts and seeds,
and chilli flakes, if using. Season with salt and pepper and devour!

WELLNESS

Unfortunately, feeling stressed and tired seems to be the norm for so many of us today that we don't even realise we're exhausted. I know because I've been there. At one point, when I was working full-time as a weather presenter and also studying to become a meteorologist, I was getting around four hours sleep a night, which wasn't doing my health any favours. Moving to Byron Bay forced me to slow down, to reconnect with nature and prioritise wellbeing as a way of life; and although a sea change isn't possible for everyone, finding little things that soothe our souls is something we should all strive to do.

Stress is at the root of so many of our health problems. When our bodies are in 'fight or flight' mode, many other essential functions shut down, including our immune and reproductive systems, and it's not something a goji berry or green smoothie is going to fix. The first step is to learn to put yourself first.

I'll be the first to admit that when life gets hectic, I struggle to fit in 'me time'. Putting the baby first is a powerful instinct, but I've come to realise that to be the best version of myself for my family, friends, work and me (see, I still put myself last!), I have to take time every day to do something that I love to do. It's taken years and a sea change, but I've finally learned to be kinder to myself, to say 'no' without feeling guilty and to switch off my phone now and again.

The latter probably seems like a small thing, but in our social media-heavy lives, switching off actually goes a long way towards helping us be happier, more relaxed and present. Don't get me wrong, I love the meaningful connections, inspiration and laughs I get from social media, but it's very easy to get caught up in other people's filtered lives and lose confidence in our own. It takes us away from the present moment. Having designated time for social media (in fact, for all online activity) and swapping just 10 minutes of 'tapping' for a walk, some meditation or a quiet cup of tea is energising and liberating. It helps us to be more mindful and connected in our own lives. *The grass isn't always greener, it's green where you water it.* So here's how I water my grass!

MOVING

When it comes to physical (and mental) health, there's no doubt that moving our bodies is important. I don't really think of it as 'exercise' but more as 'activity'. It can be a walk in nature, surfing, a run along the beach, yoga or Pilates. Some days I feel like getting my heart rate up and sweating, while other days I crave something gentle. My motivation isn't about tight abs, but about feeling absolutely wonderful. If abs happen to be a by-product of my physical activity that's awesome, but what I really value is feeling more alive and healthy. So find activities that you love and don't be afraid to try a few.

Beach walks

There are some days when I'm so caught up with chores, mama duties and work that I find it hard to leave the house. But most days, I try to fit in an afternoon walk on the beach with Archie and Darren, even if it's only 15 minutes. The ocean air and sand between our toes is both energising and grounding. I love running, but even months after giving birth I still felt quite depleted, so I stuck to the walks until I felt stronger.

Yoga

I love yoga for both its strengthening and spiritual components. Prenatal yoga was particularly helpful during pregnancy, as a gentle way of stretching, improving blood circulation and encouraging the baby to be in the optimal position for labour. It was also a lovely way for me to connect with the baby.

Pilates

My main motivation for doing Pilates is to improve and strengthen my posture, but it's also amazing for toning and lengthening the body. I love going to casual classes.

A note for mamas

During pregnancy, the body works in overdrive to support a beautiful, growing baby. During this time, there is usually a lot of love and attention on the mother, and a higher intake of nourishing foods and rest. Importantly, our society supports this and encourages mums-to-be to 'take it easy'. But when the baby is born, suddenly this all changes. Everyone's focus shifts to the baby, and mum is left to run on empty at a time when she actually needs more support than ever. The natural drive to take care of the baby's needs is essential for the child but can lead to neglect of your own health and wellbeing, which can lead to physical and emotional exhaustion.

Add to this the modern pressure to return to work (still depleted!) and to 'bounce back' to a pre-baby body, just weeks after giving birth. It took me months to recover from labour, to even walk down the street without pain. Exercise for the purpose of losing weight should be the last thing on a new mother's mind. I worked on the principle of

'9 months in – 9 months out'; in other words, that it would take *at least* 9 months for my body to adjust after childbirth, not to a pre-baby body but to a body that sustains me now as a mother. *Slowing down and nourishing oneself is not a luxury, it's vital for a mother's wellbeing.*

In our busy life schedules, nourishing ourselves can seem like 'yet another thing to do' (it does for me sometimes). But when I commit myself to napping when the baby does, cooking a wholesome meal or getting a treatment like a massage or acupuncture, it's always of enormous value.

RELAXING

For me, relaxation is switching off my mind and getting in the Zen zone. For some people, this can be exercise, while for me it's doing something slowly and peacefully.

Meditation

I studied meditation a few years ago with the wonderful Tim Brown and found it really helped me to not only relax, but also to focus my attention and make better decisions. Indeed, research suggests that just 20 minutes of meditation is as restful as 3–4 hours sleep. There are many different types of meditation, so try a few and see what feels right for you. In Tim Brown's Vedic meditation you're given a mantra, which you repeat over and over to help your mind shift from its constant surface 'chatter' to a deeper clarity, creativity, intelligence and intuition. This enables you to draw on these qualities in your everyday life. Every meditation session is different; sometimes my mind quietens to a peaceful state, while other times I'm constantly distracted by sounds and my own thoughts, such as what I'm going to eat for dinner! I just try not to allow these thoughts to frustrate me. I let them flow and keep gently returning to the mantra. No meditation is ever wasted.

Cooking

As you will have gathered, a lot of the time my greatest nourishment comes from cooking wholesome food. It's not only a circuit breaker in a busy day but very therapeutic and fulfilling, especially when the end result is delicious! Food has the greatest impact on how we look and feel, beyond any other physical activity. It's an essential investment in good health, and I believe that eating nourishing food often sparks a flow-on effect of positivity in other parts of our lives.

Coffee and crossword

This is a little bit random so fill in the blank with your favourite pastime, but for Darren and me, our daggy, much-loved daily ritual is having a coffee and doing the crossword in the morning. It's so lovely to do a little ritual every day that makes you happy. It will be a ray of sunshine no matter how busy or tired you are.

Gardening

Darren always jokes that we must be getting old, but we love pottering around the garden, planting herbs and flowers, watering things and even weeding. Yep, the country life has rubbed off. Even if you don't have a garden you can plant some beautiful edible flowers or kitchen herbs in a big pot. It's very therapeutic and so satisfying!

HEALING

When my work–life balance is out of whack and I'm doing too much and resting too little, these are some of the tools I use to fix the imbalance.

Sleep

Some people dream about holidays, but at the moment I dream about having just one good night's sleep! It's no wonder sleep is the world's number one health and beauty tonic, yet most of us treat it as an optional extra. Adults need around 7–9 hours, and the earlier you can get some shut-eye the better, as every hour before 11 pm is worth two hours afterwards. Create an environment that's inviting and peaceful, whether it be fresh sheets or a few drops of lavender on the pillow. A calming night-time ritual is also important, such as a warm bath or shower, switching off the phone, having a cup of chamomile tea or reading a book. (If you're wondering how I've managed this with a baby, the truth is I haven't – but I'm told it will get better. In the meantime, setting up a calming night-time ritual for Archie is a great help.)

Massage

Having a massage is about much more than relaxation. Releasing tension in our muscles reduces stress and helps us let go of any negative feelings we might be holding onto. This is why, sometimes, we'll have a cry or feel emotional afterwards. (I do!) By draining the lymphatic system and improving blood circulation, massage also helps to detox the body, which is why drinking plenty of water afterwards is encouraged.

Acupuncture

I'm a big fan of acupuncture. Chinese medicine is the world's oldest continually practised medical system, and acupuncture is based on the theory that *qi*, or energy, travels along pathways in our bodies called meridians, and this constant flow of energy keeps yin and yang balanced. If this energy flow is blocked, it can lead to sickness, pain or illness. Acupuncture works on releasing this *qi* and stimulates the body's natural healing response. I received acupuncture to balance out my hormones before I fell pregnant and continued regular treatments throughout my pregnancy, to support my body through all the growth and changes, and for post-labour recovery. Many of my friends have had success rebalancing their hormones and cycles, as well as falling pregnant following acupuncture sessions with a specialised practitioner, and it may have been what helped me, too. It's not a 'cure-all' though and there are many approaches towards reducing stress and treating women's issues. What works for one person may not work for another, so it's always important to seek professional advice about what treatment will work for you.

SWEET POTATO, SEAWEED AND SESAME ROSTI

SERVES 2

I've lost count of how many repurposed sweet potato rosti dishes we've had while I was perfecting this recipe. Sweet potato lacks the starchiness of white potatoes, so it needs a couple of buddies like desirees to help hold it together. The inclusion of the vibrant purple dulse seaweed is not just about adding beautiful colour and deliciousness to the rosti. It's high in vitamins (A, B, C and E) as well as iron, calcium, iodine and magnesium – minerals often lacking in our modern diets. It's a great little food to have on hand in the pantry to sprinkle onto everything from salads to soups.

1 tablespoon dulse leaf or flakes
   (see note)
250 g (about 2) desiree potatoes,
   skin on, grated
100 g (1 small) sweet potato, skin
   on, grated
2 spring onions, thinly sliced
2 teaspoons sesame seeds
zest and juice of 1 lime
sea salt and freshly ground
   black pepper
3 tablespoons ghee or
   vegetable oil
1 avocado, smashed
2 poached eggs (optional)
¼ cup sprouts (e.g. sunflower,
   mung bean, alfalfa)
coriander leaves, to serve
olive oil, for drizzling

If using dulse leaf (rather than flakes) place them in a small bowl with 60 ml (¼ cup) water and leave to soak for about 15 minutes. Squeeze out the excess water and finely chop.

Using your hands, squeeze any excess liquid from the grated desirees and transfer to a large bowl. Add the sweet potato, spring onion, sesame seeds, dulse, lime zest (not the juice yet) and mix well to combine. Season to taste.

Heat half of the ghee or oil in a 24 cm non-stick frying pan over high heat until smoking. (You want the pan to be very hot as this will 'seal' the rosti and make it nice and crisp.) Add the potato mixture and press it evenly over the base of the pan so it looks like a pancake. It will sizzle and start crisping around the edge. Cook for about 2 minutes, then reduce the heat to medium and continue cooking for a further 3 minutes. Give the pan a bit of a shake and if the whole rosti moves then you're good to slide it onto a plate.

Return the pan to a high heat and add the remaining ghee or oil. When smoking, return the rosti to the pan and cook the other side for about 2 minutes. Reduce the heat to medium and cook for a further 3 minutes.

Serve immediately in the pan topped with the smashed avocado and poached eggs, if using. Sprinkle over the sprouts and coriander leaves, drizzle with olive oil and grind over some black pepper. Once your breakfast buddy has oohed and aahed at your creation, slice it into quarters and enjoy.

NOTE

Dulse is a super-healthy type of seaweed that you can buy in most health-food stores or online. If you don't have time to soak it for 15 minutes, even a couple of minutes will make a difference.

MAKES 12 FRITTERS + 1 CUP SALSA VERDE

The first time I had fritters was at Bills in Sydney's Surry Hills and, like many before and after me, I never forgot about them. Inspired by the ridiculously sweet corn grown here in Byron, I created my own gluten-free version with a zingy salsa verde. When making the fritters, it's always best to squeeze out any excess moisture from the grated zucchini. You can omit the chilli if you're feeding kids. Store any leftover salsa in the fridge for up to three days. It's delicious with toast and avo!

kernels of 2 cooked corn cobs
1 large zucchini, coarsely grated
2 spring onions, thinly sliced
1 long green chilli, deseeded
    and finely diced
200 g (1 cup) ricotta
    (for a recipe see page 86)
3 eggs
90 g (½ cup) fine polenta
sea salt and freshly ground
    black pepper
coconut oil or ghee, for cooking

Salsa verde

½ bunch of mint, leaves picked,
    plus extra to serve
½ bunch of flat-leaf parsley,
    leaves picked, plus extra
    to serve
1 tablespoon baby capers,
    drained
1 garlic clove, chopped
1 teaspoon dijon mustard
60 ml (¼ cup) extra-virgin
    olive oil
juice of 1 lemon

To serve

crumbled Greek feta
toasted pine nuts
mixed salad leaves

To make the salsa verde, place the mint, parsley, capers, garlic and mustard in the bowl of a small food processor. Process for about 30 seconds until combined. With the motor running, pour in the oil and lemon juice and process until smooth. Transfer to a clean jar, cover and refrigerate until needed.

To make the fritters, place the corn, zucchini, spring onion and chilli in a large bowl. In another bowl or jug, beat the ricotta and eggs until smooth. Add this mixture and the polenta to the vegetables. Season and stir until just combined.

Melt a little coconut oil or ghee in a large, non-stick frying pan over medium heat. When hot, drop heaped tablespoonfuls of the mixture into the pan. Cook in batches for 2–3 minutes on each side or until golden. Transfer to a wire rack. Repeat with the remaining mixture to make 12 fritters.

Serve the fritters topped with a little feta, pine nuts and a drizzle of salsa verde. Place the salad leaves on the side and scatter over the reserved mint and parsley leaves. Finish with freshly ground black pepper.

CAFFEINE-FREE DANDY CHAI
WITH HOMEMADE NUT MILK

SERVES 4

For me, chai is the ultimate comfort drink on cold, crisp winter days and always brings back memories of an early morning road trip to Falls Creek with Darren. We were sipping on the warm, spicy milk as we drove up the mountain and it started snowing. Heaven! When I was pregnant, I came up with a caffeine-free version and it tastes just as amazing. I made it with dandelion and used Darren as my guinea pig without telling him, because he won't eat or drink anything unless it tastes good; and he loved it! I think it tastes best with homemade almond milk, but if you don't have time to make it then organic full-cream milk is also delicious. Or for a super-fast dairy-free version, macadamia milk only takes a minute to make! If your milk is fresh, the tea refrigerates well for up to three days.

5 star anise

1 teaspoon cloves

1 teaspoon chopped ginger

6 cardamom pods

1 teaspoon ground nutmeg

2 cinnamon sticks or 2 teaspoons ground cinnamon, plus extra to serve

500 ml (2 cups) filtered water

2 teaspoons dandelion tea

750 ml (3 cups) nut milk (see recipe below) or full-cream milk

1 generous tablespoon honey, or more, to taste

Nut milk

1 cup almonds soaked in filtered water overnight or 1 cup macadamia nuts

4 cups filtered water

pinch of cinnamon (optional)

pinch of sea salt (optional)

honey (optional)

To make the nut milk, drain and rinse the soaked almonds and place them in a high-powered blender with the filtered water and a little cinnamon, sea salt and honey if desired. Blend for around 1–2 minutes, until the almonds are very fine and the mixture looks like cloudy milk.

Line a strainer with muslin (or use a fine sieve) and place it over a bowl or jug. Slowly pour in the nut mixture, pressing the pulp that's left behind with a spoon to squeeze out the liquid. If using muslin, pick up the corners, draw them together and squeeze down with your other hand to get every last precious drop! (See note.)

To make macadamia milk, simply place the macadamias and filtered water in a blender with a pinch each of cinnamon and sea salt and a drop of honey, if desired, then blend. That's it! There's no pulp and no need to strain.

To make the chai, place the star anise, cloves, ginger, cardamom, nutmeg, cinnamon and water in a saucepan and bring to the boil. Reduce the heat and simmer for 10 minutes. Add the dandelion and simmer for a further 3 minutes. Strain the liquid and return to the pan. Add the milk and honey, and heat to your liking. Pour the chai into mugs, sprinkle some cinnamon on top and enjoy!

NOTES

- Store your nut milk in a sealed bottle in the fridge. It will keep for 2–3 days. Give it a shake before use.

- Don't throw out the leftover almond pulp! Spread it on a baking tray and bake for 1–1½ hours at 100°C (or use a dehydrator if you have one), giving it a stir every 30 minutes, until all of the moisture is removed. Once it cools completely you can use it as almond flour/meal. Or you can simply add the pulp to a casserole, smoothie or protein ball mix for an extra dose of good fats.

Good Matcha Morning

SERVES 2

This creamy, dreamy smoothie is such a great start to the day and is one of Darren's favourites. My friend Sam got me onto matcha, and I'm a convert! I've always loved green tea for its taste and energy boost, but matcha powder has over 100 times more antioxidants, making this smoothie a delicious and health-boosting way to get energy and nutrients first thing in the morning.

1 frozen banana
1 avocado
1 large handful of English or baby spinach leaves
1 handful of ice cubes
2 teaspoons matcha green tea powder
500 ml (2 cups) coconut milk
1 tablespoon chopped mint leaves, plus extra
    to serve
1 tablespoon maple syrup (optional)
coconut flakes, to serve

Place the banana, avocado, spinach, ice, matcha powder, coconut milk and mint leaves in a blender and whizz until smooth and creamy. Taste, and add a little maple syrup if you would like it sweeter. Transfer to glasses and top with the extra mint leaves and coconut flakes.

Blueberry Dream

SERVES 2

Blueberries are my favourite fruit to add to smoothies, as they're high in antioxidants and not too sweet, so when they're in season I freeze as many as I can. With the addition of protein and a heap of other superfoods, this smoothie seriously gets your glow on!

150 g fresh or frozen blueberries, plus extra to serve
100 g coconut yoghurt
3 tablespoons vanilla protein powder (see note on page 88)
1 tablespoon LSA (see note on page 198)
1 tablespoon chia seeds
juice and flesh of 1 young coconut
    (or 400 ml coconut water)
1 tablespoon maple syrup (optional)
coconut flakes, to serve

Place the blueberries, coconut yoghurt, protein powder, LSA, chia seeds and coconut juice and flesh in a blender and whizz until smooth and creamy. Taste, and add a little maple syrup if you would like it sweeter. Transfer to glasses and top with extra blueberries and coconut flakes.

Nutty Nana

SERVES 2

This smoothie is creamy, nutty, malty heaven. Maca is an ancient Peruvian food that's great for regulating hormones and boosting energy.

2 frozen bananas
4 medjool dates, pitted
1 teaspoon vanilla powder
2 teaspoons maca powder
1 teaspoon ground cinnamon, plus extra to serve
2 tablespoons almond butter
500 ml (2 cups) almond milk (for a recipe see page 47)

Place all of the ingredients in a blender and whizz until smooth and creamy. Transfer to glasses and top with a pinch of cinnamon.

Blueberry Dream

Good Matcha
Morning

Nutty Nana

HOW FREE RANGE
ARE YOUR EGGS?

Moving to the country has meant I'm eating more eggs than I've ever eaten in my life, and actually knowing the chooks that lay them has made me almost evangelical about this sacred food. I can't get enough of fresh, 'still warm' eggs from happy, pasture-raised chickens. Whenever friends visit from the city, they are amazed by the gorgeous bright yellow yolks and the rich taste, and always end up taking a dozen eggs home with them.

There's no doubt that the best eggs come from chickens that have the freedom to behave like real chickens: roaming fertile pastures, foraging for insects and eating scraps and organic or biodynamic grain.

Compared to factory-farmed eggs, genuine pasture-raised, free-range eggs are nutritional powerhouses containing:

› 66 per cent more vitamin A
› 4–6 more times vitamin D
› 7 times more beta carotene
› 2 times more long-chain omega-3 fatty acids
› 3 times more vitamin E

Of course, not everyone can keep chickens or has access to farmers' markets (where you can chat to the producer yourself), so we have to rely on supermarkets and green grocers to supply humanely raised eggs. Unfortunately, the legal definition of free range is only an industry code of practice that 'recommends' hens must have 'meaningful and regular' access to the outdoors at a density of no more than one hen per square metre (10,000 hens per hectare). According to the CSIRO and RSPCA, however, this figure is way too high, and their recommendation is less than 1500 chooks per hectare. And in fact, a recent Choice report found that of 183 free-range egg brands studied, 44 producers had well beyond the 1500 density (29 had 10,000 birds per hectare), 18 wouldn't disclose their densities while another 11 were either under investigation or had been fined for providing false or misleading free-range claims. So if you want the real deal, it's best to do your research online.

SUNNY

LIGHT AND UPLIFTING DISHES.
SNACKS, SALADS, PICNICS, DRINKS.

There's a reason why we all feel happier when it's sunny: the sun is our life force, nourishing the plants that nourish us. To me, sunny days mean dreamy picnics in the park with colourful salads, cheeses and iced tea. It's straw hats and warm rays kissing salty skin after a swim at the beach. It's falling asleep under a tree, book in hand. It's barbecues, pavlova and sharing food and stories with loved ones. It's the promise of hope, abundance and a plentiful harvest after days of rain or a long winter. It's the sweet floral fragrance of freesias. Just as the flowers turn their faces towards the light, so do we, drawing upon its positive energy.

PICNIC SALAD JARS

MAKES 4 × 750 ML JARS

This rainbow coloured salad is a hit at every picnic. I like to roast the beetroot, soak the lentils and make the dressing the night before so it's easy to assemble on the day. I use the whole beetroot in this salad – bulbs and leaves – which is great, seeing as we often waste the leaves and stems of many veggies.

600 g (2 bunches) baby
  beetroots with leaves
  (see note)
1 tablespoon olive oil
1 tablespoon balsamic vinegar
1 tablespoon melted and cooled
  coconut oil
1 tablespoon shredded coconut
½ teaspoon chilli flakes
½ teaspoon lemon zest
pinch of sea salt
220 g (1 cup) French-style or puy
  lentils (see note)
2 spring onions, thinly sliced
2 large oranges, peeled, pith
  removed, cut into segments
1 small fennel bulb, shaved,
  fronds reserved
120 g mixed salad leaves
125 g goat's cheese, crumbled
60 g (½ cup) walnuts, roughly
  chopped and toasted

Dressing

80 ml (⅓ cup) extra-virgin olive oil
60 ml (¼ cup) white balsamic
  vinegar
1 garlic clove, crushed
1 teaspoon dijon mustard
1 tablespoon chopped chives
pinch each of sea salt and freshly
  ground black pepper

Preheat the oven to 190°C and line two baking trays with baking paper.

Wash the beetroot and leaves well. Trim the stalks from the beetroot and set aside. Peel and quarter the beetroot and place in a bowl. Add the olive oil and vinegar, toss to coat then transfer to one of the prepared trays. Bake for 20–25 minutes or until tender. Remove from the oven and set aside to cool.

Meanwhile, remove the woody stalks and middle vein from half the beetroot leaves. Set aside the remaining leaves for another use. Dry the leaves well and tear them into pieces. Place in a bowl with the coconut oil, coconut, chilli, lemon zest and salt and toss to coat. Spread over the other prepared tray. Reduce the oven temperature to 140°C and bake for 15–20 minutes or until crisp. Remove from the oven and allow to cool for 5 minutes. Use your hands to crunch the leaves into small pieces. Store in an airtight jar ready to take to the picnic.

To make the dressing, place all of the ingredients in a glass jar with a lid and shake well.

Cook the lentils in boiling water for 15 minutes, or until tender. Drain, rinse and transfer to a bowl. Stir in the spring onion and a third of the dressing then set aside for 30 minutes or longer to allow the lentils to soak up the flavours.

To assemble, spoon the lentils into the bottom of the salad jars and top with loosely arranged beetroot, orange segments, fennel, salad leaves, goat's cheese, walnuts and the reserved fennel fronds.

Just before serving, pour over the remaining dressing, toss the salad and scatter with beetroot leaf chips.

NOTES

• Wear disposable gloves when peeling the beetroot to avoid staining your hands – unless you want hard evidence that you really *did* make this beautiful salad!

• It's best to soak the lentils in water overnight with a teaspoon of yoghurt, whey or lemon juice to ferment them a little, which not only improves their digestibility but also reduces their cooking time.

• Make sure you layer the salad quite loosely so that you can add the dressing and easily toss it in the jar. You can also make one big jar, if you prefer, or pop it in a salad bowl with a lid.

MY GO-TO SPANAKOPITA

SERVES 6

This is one of the first dishes I taught myself to cook, and it's special to me because it's my mum's favourite. (Whenever I offer to cook at Mum's, she always asks for it!) It's easy to make and produces the most delicious golden, crunchy crust. Spinach and kale are packed with iron, too, so it's a great one for kids. You can just as easily use this filling to make filo triangles if you wish.

1 tablespoon olive oil, plus extra
    for greasing
375 g filo pastry, fresh or thawed
500 g spinach, chopped
6 kale leaves, stems removed,
    chopped
1 onion, finely chopped
250 g feta
2 garlic cloves, crushed
2 spring onions, finely sliced
150 g (¾ cup) ricotta (for a recipe
    see page 86)
½ teaspoon ground nutmeg
2 tablespoons breadcrumbs
zest of ½ lemon
¼ cup mint leaves, chopped
¼ cup flat-leaf parsley leaves,
    chopped
2 eggs, beaten
100 g butter, melted
2 tablespoons sesame seeds
lemon wedges, to serve

Preheat the oven to 180°C and grease a 20 cm x 30 cm baking dish or tray with olive oil. (Don't worry if your tray is smaller, it just means that your filling will be a bit thicker.)

Place the filo sheets on a work surface and cover with a damp tea towel to prevent them from drying out.

Place the spinach and kale in a steamer over a large saucepan of boiling water and steam for 1–2 minutes or until the leaves wilt (you may need to work in batches). Set aside in a colander to drain and cool. Once cool, press the spinach and kale against the colander to squeeze out the excess water then chop into smaller pieces. (This step prevents the crust from getting soggy.)

Meanwhile, heat the olive oil in a frying pan over medium heat and cook the onion until soft and lightly golden. Set aside to cool.

Place the feta in a large bowl and rub it between your fingers to create a coarse crumb. Add the cooled onion, garlic, spring onion, ricotta, nutmeg, breadcrumbs, lemon zest, mint and parsley and mix well. (I like to do this with my hands to get a nice even texture without overmixing.) Add the spinach and kale followed by the eggs and mix again until well combined.

Using a sharp knife, halve the sheets of filo pastry. Place two sheets on a work surface and brush the top one with melted butter. Top with another two sheets of filo and again brush with butter, continuing until around half of the filo pastry has been used. Don't worry if some of the sheets tear a little as this won't matter once they're cooked. Now place the buttered sheets of filo in the tray, gently pressing them into the corners. Spoon the spinach and cheese mixture over the filo, spreading it out evenly. Butter the remaining filo sheets two sheets at a time and place them on top. Tuck in any overhanging pastry, then brush the top with butter and sprinkle with the sesame seeds.

Bake for 45 minutes or until the pastry is golden brown and crisp. If the pastry is browning too quickly, turn the heat down to 160°C and continue cooking for the remaining time. Allow the spanakopita to cool for 10 minutes before serving with lemon wedges for squeezing over. The pie makes the most satisfying crunchy sound when cut, so it's worth doing this in front of your guests!

SUMMERY PANZANELLA SALAD

SERVES 4–6

Adding sweet and decadent figs and nectarines to this traditional Tuscan panzanella salad gives it a lovely summery feel, and with the prosciutto and mozzarella it's a meal on its own. Panzanella is a great way to use stale bread, and tossing the cubes in olive oil in a bag is a foolproof way of ensuring that they stay nice and crisp. If you're sourcing your heirloom tomatoes from a farmers' market, try different coloured varieties, such as Green Tigers and Golden Yellows. This beautiful salad takes just minutes to prepare and makes a delicious accompaniment to roast or barbecued chicken.

2 tablespoons olive oil
1 garlic clove, crushed
sea salt and freshly ground
   black pepper
200 g stale sourdough bread,
   cubed
2 big handfuls of rocket
3 heirloom tomatoes, sliced
   into wedges
2 nectarines, sliced into thin
   wedges
8 slices of prosciutto, torn
6 fresh figs, torn
250 g fresh mozzarella, torn
   (or 250 g bocconcini, halved)
¼ cup small basil leaves
¼ cup small mint leaves

Dressing
60 ml (¼ cup) olive oil
3 tablespoons balsamic vinegar
1 tablespoon honey
sea salt and freshly ground
   black pepper

Place the olive oil, garlic, salt, pepper and bread in a zip-lock bag and toss until the bread is evenly coated.

Heat a frying pan over medium heat and fry the bread cubes until golden. Set aside.

Arrange the rocket on a large salad platter. Add the tomato, nectarine, prosciutto, fig and mozzarella. Sprinkle over the mint and basil leaves.

To make the dressing, whisk the oil, vinegar and honey in a small bowl. Season to taste and drizzle over the salad. Serve immediately.

MAKE YOUR OWN
DECORATIONS

To add a bespoke touch to a special occasion,
I often make my own decorations, which gives
the event a personal, earthy and boho feel.
It's also a nice bonding experience if you do it
with friends.

GARLAND GIFT

If you're organising a baby shower, hen's party or birthday for a friend, a garland is a lovely gift to create. For my baby shower, instead of gifts, I asked each of my guests to bring a trinket, bead, crystal, feather or something that was special to them. We then sat in a circle, and each person tied their treasure onto a long leather string, as they gave a positive affirmation to the baby. Now I have a beautiful garland filled with personal treasures and positive energy hanging in the baby's room. Doing this was the highlight of everyone's day and it's an heirloom I'll treasure forever.

DREAMCATCHERS

There's something very calm and serene about dreamcatchers. People always seem to be drawn to them and they look beautiful hanging off tree branches, swaying in the breeze.

Materials

› a metal or wooden ring
   (or make one from garden vine)
› string or twine made from leather,
   jute or any natural fibre
› scissors
› shells, feathers, beads and crystals

You can buy wooden and metal rings from craft stores, but I love to make my own using whatever vine I can find in the garden. I arrange the vines in different-sized circles, tie the ends with string and dry them in the sun to harden.

Cut a length of string about 10 times the circumference of your ring. Tie one end to the ring leaving a loop (this is your hanging loop). Now it's time to weave the web. Take your string and loosely loop it over the hoop 2–3 cm from your knot, and pull it through the space between the string and the hoop. Pull it tight. Repeat this stitch at evenly spaced intervals until you reach the top of your ring again, making sure you pull the string tight after each stitch. You have now completed the first round of the web. Now, weave the string around again, but this time place the stitch in the centre of each section of tightened string, pulling the string tight between each stitch – the string will be pulled towards the centre of the ring forming a web.

Continue this method, making the circle smaller and smaller, until you reach the middle of the ring, then attach a bead, crystal or feather. (You can also attach a bead between each stitch, too.) Weave some beads and attach some feathers on varying lengths of leather and then tie these to the bottom of the ring.

BUNTING

It's festive and beautiful, especially if you make it yourself using your favourite colours. For something a little more chic you can try using fabric and ribbon.

Materials

› different coloured paper or fabric
› guillotine or scissors
› hole punch
› natural twine or ribbon

Cut your paper into triangles with a guillotine, or use sharp scissors to cut triangles of fabric. (I made mine in two different sizes, 25 cm and 30 cm, but feel free to make them whatever size you prefer.) Punch or cut a hole in the two top corners of each triangle and thread the twine or ribbon through. Easy and gorgeous!

HANGING FLOWERS ON A BRANCH

This makes a stunning backdrop for a dessert table, and I guarantee there'll be lots of people taking Instagram photos!

Materials

› 1–1.5 metre long tree branch
› 20 flowers with sturdy stems (e.g. roses)
› string
› rope or heavy twine
› scissors

Pick a sturdy fallen branch from your garden or a nearby park (fallen limbs from eucalypts are great to use). Cut 20 pieces of string at different lengths, and tie them to the branch about 2–3 cm apart. Then randomly tie your flowers to the strings to create a beautiful 'curtain' of flowers. Cut a 2 metre length of rope, and tie it to each end of the branch to create a hanging loop. Hang the branch and let the flowers flow in the wind. Gorgeous!

This is the potato salad that the Polish mamas make when they need to pull out the big guns for Christmas, Easter, birthdays and special barbecues. I have such fond memories associated with this salad – dicing up all the veggies on wooden boards in the backyard was the only job my dad, sister and I had to do while Mum would single-handedly whip up the other 25 dishes. (We always made Dad do the onions!) Once the salad was dressed with special mayo to my dad's taste, it was shaped into a perfect dome and put in the fridge until ready. But every time my mum took it out to serve there was always a hole in it where someone had sneakily gone in for a spoonful! It used to drive her mad. Everyone looks forward to a Polish gathering because they know this salad will make an appearance and despite using identical ingredients, no two taste the same. Every Polish mama has her own brand. And secretly, everyone always thinks their mum's is the best one. Now that I've had Archie, this is mine.

4 large desiree potatoes,
    unpeeled
6 carrots, unpeeled
4 eggs, at room temperature
5 gherkins, cut into 5 mm cubes
    and drained (for a recipe see
    page 222)
2 small brown onions, finely
    chopped
1 green apple, peeled, cored
    and cut into 5 mm cubes
1 x 400 g can green peas, drained
    and rinsed

Special mayonnaise
2 egg yolks
1 teaspoon dijon mustard, plus
    extra to taste
2 tablespoons white wine vinegar
juice of 1 lemon
250 ml (1 cup) grapeseed oil
sea salt and freshly ground
    black pepper

Place the potatoes and carrots in a large saucepan, cover with water and bring to the boil over medium–high heat. Cook until tender. Drain and set aside to cool.

Meanwhile, place the eggs in a saucepan of cold water and bring to the boil. Cook for 8 minutes, then drain and run under cold water to stop the cooking process. Once cool, peel and dice the eggs into 5 mm cubes.

When the potatoes and carrots have cooled completely, peel and cut them into 5 mm cubes. Transfer to a large salad bowl along with the egg, gherkin, onion, apple and peas.

To make the special mayonnaise, place the egg yolks, mustard, vinegar and lemon juice in a jug and whisk with a stick blender for 1 minute. Continue whisking while slowly adding the grapeseed oil down the inside of the jug in a thin stream until the mixture emulsifies. When all the oil is incorporated your mixture will have a beautiful, silky, creamy consistency.

Stir about 4 tablespoons of the mayonnaise through the salad until the ingredients are well coated. Have a taste, then add some more mustard if you like and season to taste. No one really knows how much special mayo anyone puts in. This is the part that makes it your own.

NOTE

If you don't feel like making your own mayo, use a good-quality whole-egg mayonnaise and just add a little extra dijon mustard, to taste.

CRUNCHY VEG AND QUINOA SALAD WITH CASHEW PESTO

SERVES 4–6 + ABOUT 1 CUP LEFTOVER PESTO

I'm pretty sure it's quinoa that got me to Machu Picchu. My guides swore by it as the 'Peruvian penicillin' when I got sick during the four-day hike up the Inca Trail, so I had it in porridge, soups and stews. It worked and I became a bit obsessed with it. But it was the early 2000s, and when I got back home I couldn't find it anywhere but the odd health-food store. How times have changed! Here, I've combined this wonderful grain with some other legendary foods like goji berries, broccoli, cauliflower and pickled onion. One of my favourite things about fermented vegetables, apart from the probiotic benefits, is the zingy taste they add to salads. If you don't have any to hand, you can 'quickle' (a delightful term I've borrowed from Matt Preston!) certain vegetables by soaking them in vinegar for as little as 30 minutes to a few hours, like the onions in this salad. It not only brings the salad to life, but the onions turn a beautiful pink colour.

1 red onion, thinly sliced

125 ml (½ cup) red wine vinegar

2 tablespoons vegetable oil
    or ghee

½ medium head of cauliflower,
    florets finely chopped

1 medium head of broccoli, florets
    finely chopped

2 tablespoons apple cider vinegar

2 tablespoons goji berries

1 tablespoon freshly squeezed
    orange juice

190 g (1 cup) tri-coloured quinoa,
    cooked and chilled (see note)

2 tablespoons pumpkin seeds,
    toasted, to serve

handful of basil leaves, to serve

Cashew pesto

75 g (½ cup) unsalted cashews

60 g parmesan, finely diced

1 garlic clove, crushed

1 large bunch of basil, leaves
    picked

juice of 1 lemon

125 ml (½ cup) avocado oil

Combine the onion and red wine vinegar in a glass jar or bowl and set aside to 'quickle' for at least 30 minutes, but preferably 3–4 hours.

To make the pesto, place the cashews, parmesan and garlic in a food processor and blitz for about 20 seconds. Add the basil leaves and process for another 20 seconds. While the motor is running, pour in the lemon juice and oil, and process for about 30 seconds until smooth. Transfer to a bowl, cover and set aside.

Heat the oil or ghee in a large frying pan over high heat. Add the cauliflower and broccoli and cook for 1–2 minutes, stirring, until the broccoli is bright in colour but still crunchy. Drizzle with the apple cider vinegar and remove from the heat. Transfer to a large bowl and set aside for 15 minutes to cool.

Meanwhile soak the goji berries in the orange juice for 15 minutes to slightly rehydrate.

Add the cooked quinoa, goji berries and ½ cup of the pesto to the vegetables and toss to combine. Transfer to a serving platter and top with the pumpkin seeds, basil leaves and pickled onion.

NOTES

- To cook quinoa, first rinse the grains thoroughly under running water until the water runs clear. Then, ideally, soak them overnight in a bowl of warm water and a teaspoon of acid like lemon juice to help make them more digestible. When you're ready to use them, rinse them again and drain. Place the quinoa in a saucepan and measure out 1½ cups water to 1 cup soaked quinoa (1¾ cups water to 1 cup rinsed but not soaked quinoa). Bring to the boil, reduce the heat and simmer, covered, for 15–20 minutes until the water has been absorbed. Remove from the heat and allow to rest, covered, for a further 10 minutes.

- I always like to make extra pesto, as it's so handy to have as a snack, to add to a salad or stir through pasta. Store the leftovers in a tightly sealed container in the fridge for up to 7 days.

FARM SALAD WITH RICOTTA AND SALSA VERDE

SERVES 4 + ½ CUP LEFTOVER SALSA

When we were little, we used to love it when Dad would make us dinner while Mum was studying. He'd make us a simple meal of chopped gherkins with cottage cheese, and we loved it! If we ate it all, he'd make us a 'Nutella calzone', which was basically just Nutella on a piece of bread folded in half. The farm produce here in Byron is so amazing that sometimes the best thing to do is as little as possible and ensure that nothing goes to waste! Inspired by Dad's dinners, I've slightly pickled the veggies by tossing them in apple cider vinegar and then used the carrot tops and radish leaves to make a zingy salsa verde that is bursting with flavour. If you can get your hands on heirloom veggies from a farmers' market they work best in this salad for their freshness, colour, intense flavour and crunch. You can serve this as a starter, using the veggies to scoop up the cheese, or as a salad.

1 bunch of small baby carrots
  with tops
1 bunch of radishes with leaves
250 g heirloom cherry tomatoes
  (or 2 truss tomatoes)
2 cucumbers
2 tablespoons apple cider vinegar
1 teaspoon salt
500 g homemade ricotta
  (see page 86)

Carrot and radish leaf salsa verde

1½ cups chopped carrot top
  leaves and radish leaves
1 gherkin, roughly chopped
  (for a recipe see page 222)
1 cup flat-leaf parsley
¼ cup dill fronds
1 garlic clove, crushed
1 tablespoon dijon mustard
3 tablespoons apple cider vinegar
1 tablespoon capers
½ tablespoon honey
4 tablespoons olive oil
sea salt and freshly ground
  black pepper

Cut the tops off the carrots and radishes, trim the stalks (carrot stalks are very bitter) and set aside for the salsa. Now chop your carrots, radishes, tomatoes and cucumbers so they're chunky enough to scoop up the ricotta. Place them all in a bowl with the vinegar and salt, and set aside to 'quickle' for about 30 minutes (or as long as you have).

Place all of the salsa ingredients except the salt and pepper in a food processor and blitz until it forms a runny paste. Add more olive oil if necessary until it reaches your desired consistency. Season with salt and pepper to taste. If it's too acidic, add a little more honey, half a teaspoon at a time.

Place your ricotta on a large serving dish and arrange your vegetables over the top in a nice colourful, mess. Generously drizzle over the salsa verde. If you're entertaining, encourage your guests to eat with their hands; it always tastes better that way!

NOTE

Store the leftover salsa verde in a sealed container in the fridge and use as a delicious addition to salads.

BROWN RICE VEGGIE SUSHI ROLLS WITH WASABI-LIME MAYONNAISE

SERVES 3–4

This recipe is inspired by Doma, a gorgeous little Japanese cafe in the Byron hinterland. I particularly love their brown rice sushi rolls, so I decided to come up with my own version. I'd actually never made sushi rolls before because I was worried they might be too difficult, but I'm pleased to say that I was wrong and even if they are a bit wonky, they look gorgeous on a platter. If you have the time, it's so worth making the wasabi–lime mayo because you can really taste the difference, though feel free to add wasabi paste and a squeeze of lime to store-bought mayo if you don't.

300 g (1½ cups) brown rice
3 tablespoons rice wine vinegar
6 nori sheets (19 cm x 21 cm)
soy sauce, to serve
pickled ginger, to serve

Sweet potato and haloumi filling

1 sweet potato, cut lengthways into 5 mm thick matchsticks
2 tablespoons grapeseed oil
2 tablespoons sesame seeds
80 g haloumi, cut into 3 mm thick slices
1 cucumber, cut lengthways into 5 mm thick matchsticks

Veggie patch filling

50 g tempeh, cut into 3 mm thick slices
1 carrot, cut lengthways into 5 mm matchsticks
1 avocado, cut lengthways into 5 mm thick slices
½ red capsicum, deseeded, cut lengthways into 5 mm slices
3 spring onions, sliced into 8 cm lengths

Wasabi–lime mayonnaise

2 egg yolks
1 teaspoon dijon mustard
2 tablespoons rice wine vinegar
juice of 1 lime
250 ml (1 cup) grapeseed oil
4 teaspoons wasabi paste
sea salt and white pepper

Place the brown rice in a bowl, cover with cold water and swirl the rice around with your hands until the water is cloudy, then drain. Repeat this process until the water is clean. Be sure to drain your cloudy water into a bucket so you can use it to water your plants! Place the rice in a saucepan with 560 ml (2¼ cups) of water and let it soak for a couple of hours.

Preheat the oven to 180°C and line a baking tray with baking paper.

When you're ready to cook the rice, cover the pan and bring it to the boil over medium heat. Reduce the heat to low and simmer for 15–20 minutes. When all of the liquid has been absorbed, take the rice off the heat (keep the lid on) and leave it to steam for a further 10 minutes. Gently fold in the rice wine vinegar and stir it occasionally while it cools. It will be a little sticky.

While the rice is cooking, place the sweet potato on the prepared tray, drizzle with 1 tablespoon of the oil, sprinkle with sesame seeds and roast in the oven for 15–20 minutes. Remove from the oven and set aside to cool.

Meanwhile, heat the remaining tablespoon of oil in a frying pan and fry the haloumi and tempeh for about 3 minutes on each side until golden brown.

To make the mayonnaise, combine the egg yolks, mustard, vinegar and lime juice in a bowl and whisk with a stick blender for 1 minute. Continue whisking while slowly adding the grapeseed oil in a thin stream down the inside of the bowl until the mixture emulsifies and you have a beautiful, silky, creamy consistency. Add the wasabi, ½ teaspoon at a time, until you get the heat you like, then season with salt and white pepper.

Place a nori sheet on a sushi rolling mat and pat an even layer of rice over the nori, leaving about 5 cm uncovered along the top edge. Arrange a line of either the sweet potato and haloumi filling or the veggie patch filling about 2 cm away from the bottom edge of the nori. Drizzle with wasabi mayonnaise.

Pick up the edge of the rolling mat that's closest to you, fold it over the vegetables and roll to make a thick cylinder. With wet fingertips, brush the bare edge of the nori and seal. Gently squeeze the roll in the mat to compact it tightly. Repeat with the remaining nori sheets and fillings. Let the rolls rest for a few minutes and then cut each roll into 4–6 pieces. Serve with soy sauce, pickled ginger and smugness.

FALAFEL

I fell in love with falafel during a holiday in Israel, where I must have had them at least twice a day! Byron Bay is also home to some excellent falafel, which inspired me to start making them at home. I love to eat them with chopped gherkins, hummus, eggplant dip and Israeli salad – a delicious Middle Eastern feast! I strongly encourage you to use dried chickpeas rather than canned ones because they're not only more nutritious, but also provide a much better consistency for the falafel. But don't worry, this doesn't mean extra work or cooking. You simply need to start this recipe a day before to soak the chickpeas, but you don't need to pre-cook them as they'll cook when you fry them, so this literally takes minutes to prepare. I add a tablespoon of yoghurt, whey or lemon juice to mine so they ferment a little which makes them more digestible and flavoursome. Falafel are also delicious with tahini and chilli sauce.

400 g (2 cups) dried chickpeas

1 tablespoon yoghurt, whey or lemon juice

1 onion, finely chopped

4 garlic cloves

¼ cup flat-leaf parsley leaves, chopped

½ cup coriander leaves, chopped

4 tablespoons flour (any kind)

1 egg, lightly beaten

1 teaspoon baking soda

3 teaspoons ground cumin

2 teaspoons smoked paprika

2 teaspoons sea salt

¼ teaspoon freshly ground black pepper

¼ teaspoon cayenne pepper

grapeseed oil, for brushing

To serve

hummus

chopped gherkins, (for a recipe see page 222)

Israeli salad (see page 81)

Smoky eggplant dip (see page 80)

Place the chickpeas in a bowl with plenty of water and a tablespoon of yoghurt, whey or lemon juice. Cover with a tea towel and leave to soak overnight. They will double in size so you'll end up with about 4 cups of chickpeas.

The next morning, wash the chickpeas and drain well. Transfer to a food processor along with the rest of the ingredients except the oil, and blitz until you get a coarse paste. Don't overdo it as you don't want to end up with mush – texture is important. Spoon the mixture into a bowl and refrigerate for a couple of hours. This helps to bind it together when you shape it into balls.

Preheat the oven to 180°C. Line a baking tray with baking paper and brush with oil.

Take ¼ cup of the mixture (about 2 heaped tablespoons) and form into a ball. If the mixture is too wet, add a little more flour. Gently place on the baking paper and press down to form a patty 1–2 cm thick. Repeat with the remaining mixture. Brush the tops of the falafel patties with some oil and then place in the oven to bake for 25–30 minutes or until golden brown. Turn the falafel halfway through, so that both sides are crisp and golden brown. Enjoy immediately with hummus, chopped gherkins, my Israeli salad and Smoky eggplant dip (see overleaf), or some fresh pita and your favourite dips and side dishes.

NOTES

- Falafel can be shallow-fried in a skillet over medium heat for about 4 minutes on each side, but baking is easier and uses less oil, and they turn out just as crisp.
- You can keep the cooked falafel in the fridge for up to 3 days.

SMOKY EGGPLANT DIP

MAKES 1¼ CUPS

This smoky eggplant dip is such a delicious starter, you'll need to make a double batch if you're feeding more than four. You can keep the presentation beautifully simple with just a drizzle of olive oil, a pinch of smoked paprika and a smattering of coriander leaves. But if you want to go the extra mile, it looks particularly impressive with pomegranate seeds and toasted nuts such as pine nuts or almonds. Trust me, it will be all over Insta! It's the perfect companion to fresh vegetables, pita, salads and falafel (see my Falafel and Israeli salad recipes on page 78 and opposite). I even love it on toasted sourdough with some sliced tomato and a poached egg. Don't be afraid to let the skin go black when you char the eggplant, as you'll discard this part and devour the gorgeous fleshy part inside. It's faster to do it straight over a flame, but you can also use a chargrill pan. The smoky taste always makes me feel like I'm on some exotic holiday – well, until the baby cries! Luckily, it can be enjoyed immediately and keeps well in the fridge for up to three days.

1 large eggplant (about 400 g)

1 tablespoon Greek yoghurt

2 tablespoons tahini

½ garlic clove, finely grated

1 tablespoon lemon juice

½ teaspoon smoked paprika, plus extra to serve

½ teaspoon sumac

½ teaspoon ground cumin

1 teaspoon sea salt

2 tablespoons olive oil

If you have a gas stovetop, light one of the burners and set it to medium heat. Now put the eggplant on top of the flame and let it cook for about 10 minutes, using tongs to turn it frequently, until the skin is blackened. Alternatively, heat a chargrill pan over medium–high heat and cook the eggplant for about 20 minutes, turning it often, until charred and soft. Set aside to cool.

When cool enough to handle, halve the eggplant lengthways and scoop the flesh out into a colander, squeezing it gently to remove any excess liquid. Once it's completely cool, transfer to a food processor along with the yoghurt, tahini, garlic, lemon juice, paprika, sumac, cumin and salt, and pulse until you get a smooth paste.

To serve, spoon the eggplant dip into a bowl, drizzle with olive oil and garnish with a sprinkle of paprika

ISRAELI SALAD

SERVES 4

I was inspired to make this salad after my holiday in Israel where it was the fresh accompaniment to almost every meal, and I've been making it ever since. It's fast and fresh and pairs perfectly with fish and falafel. I love having the leftovers for breakfast or lunch with a poached egg. The salad has less chance of getting soggy if the tomatoes and cucumbers are deseeded, but I don't like to waste them, so if I'm eating it right away I keep them in. It's best to chop and dress it just before serving for maximum crispness.

2 tomatoes (about 500 g),
   diced into 5 mm cubes
3 Lebanese cucumbers (about
   500 g), diced into 5 mm cubes
2 spring onions, thinly sliced
¼ cup mint leaves, finely chopped
¼ cup flat-leaf parsley leaves,
   finely chopped
juice of 1 lemon
2 tablespoons olive oil
1 teaspoon sea salt

Mix the tomato, cucumber, spring onion, mint and parsley in a bowl.
Toss through the lemon juice, olive oil and sea salt and enjoy immediately.

SERVES 4

We had a bounty of cauliflower towards the end of one winter, so I had to get creative with ways to use it all up. Spring vegetables, such as asparagus, were just coming in, and so this cauli pizza was born. While I'm totally happy to eat traditional dough, this cauliflower version is light, simple to make and saves the kitchen floor from being covered in flour! It happens to be gluten free, too. If you can get your hands on a creamy burrata, it is simply phenomenal oozing in the centre of the pizza or torn over the top.

600 g cauliflower florets

2 eggs, beaten

25 g (⅓ cup) finely grated
parmesan

sea salt and freshly ground
black pepper

170 g asparagus, trimmed and
sliced diagonally into thirds

400 g mixed heirloom tomatoes,
halved lengthways

4 marinated artichoke hearts
with stems, drained and halved
lengthways

1 small red onion, thinly sliced
into rounds

2 tablespoons olive oil

2 tablespoons lemon juice

1 burrata, to serve (see note)

Zucchini pesto

1 zucchini, roughly chopped

40 g (¼ cup) almonds

2 garlic cloves, peeled

½ cup basil leaves

2 teaspoons finely grated
lemon zest

2 tablespoons lemon juice

20 g (¼ cup) finely grated
parmesan

60 ml (¼ cup) olive oil

sea salt and freshly ground
black pepper

Preheat the oven to 220°C. Line two large baking trays with baking paper.

Place the cauliflower in the bowl of a food processor and pulse until finely chopped (about the size of rice grains). Transfer to a large bowl with the egg and parmesan. Season to taste and stir until well combined. Spread the cauliflower mixture over one of the prepared trays to form a rectangle 5 mm thick. Bake for 30 minutes or until cooked through and golden.

Meanwhile, place the asparagus, tomato, artichoke, onion, oil and lemon juice in a large bowl. Season to taste and toss until well coated. Spread the mixture evenly over the remaining prepared tray. Bake for 15 minutes or until the vegetables are just tender and starting to turn light golden.

While the base and topping are cooking, make the zucchini pesto. Combine all of the ingredients in a food processor and process until smooth, adding a tablespoon of water to loosen the mixture if needed. Season to taste.

To serve, spread the pesto evenly over the hot pizza base, then top with the hot vegetable mixture. Place the burrata in the middle and make a small incision, so the inside oozes out. Slice and enjoy!

NOTES

- Burrata is an Italian cheese made with a firm layer of mozzarella on the outside and a delicious, creamy cheese inside. It's heaven!

- For a no-cook topping, carefully toss together 4 sliced heirloom tomatoes, 1 very thinly sliced green zucchini, 1 very thinly sliced yellow zucchini, 1 cup snow pea tendrils, 1 tablespoon avocado oil and 2 tablespoons lemon juice. Season to taste. Spread the pesto over the cooked base and top with the freshly chopped vegetables and the burrata.

MAKE YOUR OWN
SOLAR INFUSED HERBAL OIL

Solar-infused herbal oil sounds so fancy doesn't it? Yet, this natural skin remedy is so simple and cheap to make! I got this recipe from my friends Amanda and Andrew at Church Farm General Store in the small town of Billinudgel. They make the most amazing natural soap by hand and many of the ingredients they use, such as medicinal flowers, are grown on their property, where they've turned an old timber church into their beautiful family home.

I hadn't heard about solar-infused herbal oils before meeting Amanda, but basically they're nourishing oils infused with the healing and medicinal properties of herbs. They are much gentler than essential oils, so can be used topically, and they look stunning while they're infusing on the windowsill!

I love rosemary for its soothing and antibacterial qualities, but you can also try lavender, chamomile, calendula or lemon balm – the possibilities are endless.

You can also make solar-infused oils for cooking with herbs and spices, such as lemongrass, oregano and thyme. They're absolutely delicious!

Rosemary solar-infused olive oil

You can use a few drops in the bath, on its own as a super-hydrating moisturiser, or as an ointment or wound salve.

MAKES 1 X 500 ML JAR

handful of dried rosemary sprigs (or herbs or flowers of your choice)
400 ml olive oil (see note)
sunshine
patience

Place the rosemary sprigs in a clean 500 ml jar. (If using fresh herbs, dry them overnight to remove excess moisture.)

Pour the olive oil into the jar, making sure the herbs are covered by at least 3 cm of oil and there is 3 cm of space at the top of the jar (in case the flowers or herbs need room to expand). Give the herbs and oil a good stir and pop the lid on.

Store the jar on a sunny and warm windowsill, shaking once per day. After 4–6 weeks, strain the oil using a sieve, muslin cloth or a nut milk bag. Store the infused oil in a dark place either in the same jar or a glass bottle (for easy pouring).

NOTE

You can use other carrier oils such as grapeseed (for cooking) and jojoba or sweet almond (for skin ointments).

RISOTTO WITH PEAS AND HOMEMADE RICOTTA

SERVES 4 + MAKES ABOUT 500 G RICOTTA

Before we moved to Byron and started getting our milk straight from the dairy, the idea of making my own cheese had never occurred to me, but I'm so glad I gave it a go because it is so easy and satisfying. One of the by-products of making ricotta is whey, which often ends up in the fridge and inevitably goes to waste. Not any more! You can use it for this delicious risotto recipe or instead of the buttermilk in my scones recipe on page 233. The whey creates the most gorgeous, creamy texture. This recipe is definitely a family favourite.

1 tablespoon olive oil

100 g pancetta, thinly sliced

50 g unsalted butter

1 onion, thinly sliced

2 garlic cloves, crushed

750 ml–1 litre (3–4 cups) whey (from the ricotta)

300 g (1½ cups) arborio rice

bunch of watercress, leaves picked, stems reserved

sea salt and freshly ground black pepper

100 g peas, fresh or frozen and thawed

zest of 1 lemon and juice of ½ lemon

2 tablespoons finely chopped flat-leaf parsley leaves

50 g parmesan, grated

Ricotta

2 litres (8 cups) full-cream milk

pinch of sea salt

3 tablespoons apple cider vinegar

To make the ricotta, heat the milk and salt in a large saucepan until it reaches 85–90°C on a kitchen thermometer and you see tiny bubbles forming at the edge of the pan. Remove the pan from the heat. Add the vinegar, stirring gently for about 1 minute or until curds start forming (those curds are your cheese!). Cover the saucepan with a tea towel and let it rest for about 30 minutes while the curds do their thing.

Line a colander with muslin and place it over a bowl. Using a slotted spoon, transfer the ricotta to the colander and leave it to drain for about an hour. If the liquid (whey) in the pan still looks quite milky, reheat it to 85–90°C and add some more vinegar (about a tablespoon) and continue to skim the curds until the whey is yellowish in colour. Reserve the whey (there will be about 3–4 cups) and set aside 100 g of the ricotta to make the risotto. Store the leftover ricotta in the fridge for up to 4 days. (It's delicious with honey and herbs, such as lemon thyme or rosemary.)

To make the risotto, heat the olive oil in a large, heavy-based saucepan over medium heat. Add the pancetta and cook for about 5 minutes, or until golden and crisp. Remove from the pan and drain on paper towel. Return the pan to the heat and melt the butter. Add the onion and garlic and sauté for about 7 minutes, or until the onion is soft and translucent.

Meanwhile, reheat the whey over medium–low heat until hot but not boiling.

Add the rice to the onion and garlic and stir for a couple of minutes until the rice is nicely coated. Now make yourself comfortable with your favourite beverage, since you'll be adding the whey to the risotto ladle by ladle and stirring for the next 20 minutes. (I really enjoy this part, it's quite meditative!) Start by adding a ladle of hot whey to the rice, stirring often but not constantly until the liquid is absorbed. Continue ladling in the whey, allowing each ladleful to be absorbed before adding the next one, until the rice is cooked to your liking. It should be al dente and creamy. When the rice is almost ready, stir through the watercress stems and cook for about 1 minute or until soft. Season to taste with salt and pepper.

Stir through the peas, lemon zest and parsley. Very gently stir through 100 g of the ricotta and the lemon juice. Serve topped with the pancetta, watercress leaves and freshly grated parmesan.

CHERRY AND ALMOND SUMMER TART

SERVES 8–10

It doesn't matter what I'm shopping for, if there's a bunch of cherries looking at me I have to get them. One of my favourite ways of indulging in them, especially when there's an abundance during summer, is in a delicious tart. I absolutely love frangipane tarts, but they can be a bit of a work-up with the shortcrust pastry. This is the tart I make when I want the experience of a delicious, chewy, gooey frangipane without the fuss. It looks and tastes divine! Cherries are the perfect accompaniment to the coconut and almonds, but you can use any berries, apples or whatever fruit is in season.

200 g (2 cups) almond meal
60 g (⅔ cup) desiccated coconut
200 g caster sugar
½ teaspoon ground cinnamon
4 eggs, beaten
1½ teaspoons vanilla extract
½ teaspoon almond essence
200 g unsalted butter, melted
  and cooled
225 g pitted cherries (see note)
thickened cream or crème fraîche,
  to serve (optional)
edible flowers, to serve (optional)

Preheat the oven to 180°C. Grease a 23 cm round spring-form tin and line it with baking paper.

Place the almond meal, coconut, sugar and cinnamon in a bowl and mix until well combined.

In another bowl, mix together the eggs, vanilla, almond essence and butter. Add the wet mixture to the dry mixture and stir well to combine. Pour into the prepared tin and gently press the cherries into the top.

Bake for 45 minutes. Cool in the tin on a wire rack. Serve on its own or with thickened cream or crème fraîche. It looks particularly pretty topped with edible elderflowers or chamomile flowers.

NOTE

If you don't have a pitter, it's very easy to pit your cherries using a paperclip. Bend open the paperclip and push one of the rounded ends into the stem end of the cherry. Twist it around the pit and pull it out.

Chocolate and Vanilla Protein Balls

MAKES 12

I came up with these when I was breastfeeding Archie – clearly I needed the energy! It only took me about 5–10 minutes to whip them up with him in a sling, so they're really easy. These super-nutritious protein balls make a great snack mid-morning or whenever you need a pick-me-up. They've definitely saved me from getting 'hangry' many a time! Daz reckons they're the best protein balls he's tasted and heads straight to the fridge to tuck into them after a surf. They're really chocolaty, malty and a bit gooey. Heaven!

8 medjool dates, pitted
3 tablespoons coconut oil
2 tablespoons almond butter
3 tablespoons cacao powder
1 tablespoon cacao nibs, plus extra for rolling
2 tablespoons LSA (see note on page 198)
2 tablespoons vanilla protein powder (see note)
¼ teaspoon vanilla extract or powder
1 tablespoon shredded coconut, plus extra for rolling
1 tablespoon chia seeds

Place all of the ingredients in a food processor and blitz until thoroughly combined. If the mixture seems dry, add a little more coconut oil or almond butter. If it seems too wet, add a 'dry' ingredient like LSA. Use a spatula to scoop the mixture into a bowl.

Combine the extra cacao nibs and shredded coconut and sprinkle them onto a plate.

With damp hands, roll heaped tablespoonfuls of the mixture into balls then coat them evenly in the cacao and coconut mixture. Refrigerate for at least 1 hour to set then enjoy! These will keep in a sealed container in the fridge for up to 7 days (if they don't get eaten first!).

Golden Fig and Turmeric Moon Balls

MAKES 15

This recipe is not only packed with good oils, fats and protein but also contains the super-spice turmeric, which is believed to help with everything from poor digestion to colds. The best part is that these balls taste truly delicious and are *very* easy to make.

225 g (1½ cups) cashews
4–5 dried figs
2 tablespoons vanilla protein powder (see note)
1 tablespoon coconut oil
1 tablespoon almond or peanut butter
1 tablespoon vanilla extract
1 tablespoon honey
1 tablespoon white chia seeds
1 tablespoon ground turmeric

Before you get started, make sure you're not wearing your favourite white tee or using your favourite tea towel, because turmeric is one of those spices that stains! Once you're sorted, place ½ cup of the cashews in a food processor and pulse until finely chopped. Transfer to a plate and set aside.

Place the remaining ingredients in the food processor and blitz until the cashews are coarsely ground and the mixture is well combined. If the mixture seems too oily to form into balls, add a little bit more of a 'dry' ingredient, such as protein powder. If it's too dry, add a little more of a 'wet' ingredient, such as coconut oil. Scrape the mixture into a bowl and refrigerate for 30 minutes to firm up.

With damp hands, roll heaped tablespoonfuls of the mixture into balls, then roll them in the chopped cashews. Refrigerate for at least an hour and enjoy!

NOTE

I use Amazonia Raw Fermented Paleo Protein with vanilla and lucuma flavour, which is plant-based and sugar-free.

MINI MATCHA PAVLOVAS WITH
COCONUT YOGHURT AND FRESH FRUITS

MAKES 12

My inspiration for a matcha pavlova with fresh fruits came from an impromptu dinner party at my friend Palisa Anderson's house here in Byron. Chefs Analiese Gregory (Bar Brosé) and Trish Greenwood (Brae) happened to be in town and whipped up the most incredible meal using locally sourced produce. The *piece de resistance* was a pavlova using eggs from Palisa's chooks and a rainbow of in-season fruits from neighbouring farm, Picone Exotics. John Picone's orchard is often described as a garden of Eden by anyone lucky enough to visit. He even manages to grow vanilla, pepper and cocoa, which is virtually unheard of in our climate! We don't know how he does it, but it might be a mixture of his incredible passion, encyclopedic knowledge and maybe even the crystals he buries in the soil. I've always made my pavlovas with traditional whipped cream, but this matcha-flavoured meringue lends itself beautifully to coconut yoghurt, hence the dairy-free version. The great thing about pavlova is that if anything goes wrong, you just turn it into Eton mess. Win-win!

6 egg whites

¼ teaspoon cream of tartar

pinch of salt (see note)

330 g (1½ cups) caster sugar

1½ teaspoons matcha powder
(see note)

2 teaspoons white vinegar

350 g coconut yoghurt, to serve

pulp of 3 passionfruit

2 starfruit (carambola), sliced

1 dragon fruit (see note)

6 lychees, peeled, pitted and
halved

small punnet of mulberries
(optional)

edible flowers, to serve (optional)

Heat the oven to 120°C. Line two baking trays with baking paper and draw six 8-cm circles 3 cm apart on each piece of paper.

Place the egg whites and cream of tartar in the bowl of a stand mixer and beat on high speed for 1–2 minutes until soft peaks form. With the motor still running, add the salt then the sugar 1 tablespoon at a time, allowing each tablespoon to dissolve before adding the next one. Continue beating for 7–8 minutes until the mixture is thick and glossy. Rub a small amount of mixture between your thumb and forefinger – it should feel smooth and not grainy. Add the matcha powder and vinegar and continue beating for a further 1 minute until combined. Dollop large spoonfuls of the mixture to fill each circle on the baking paper, dragging the meringue mixture upwards to form peaks.

Bake for 2 hours until firm to the touch, rotating the trays halfway through cooking. Turn the oven off and place a tea towel in the door to keep it ajar. Allow the meringues to cool completely in the oven.

Spoon the coconut yoghurt onto the cooled pavlovas. Top with the fresh fruits and edible flowers, if using, and serve immediately.

NOTES

- Don't omit the salt – it helps stabilise the egg white. And remember, moisture is the enemy of the pavlova, so avoid making it on very humid days. Also, fat will spoil a pavlova, so make sure your implements are free of grease and that there is no yolk left in your separated eggs.

- Matcha is basically finely ground green tea but has 137 times more antioxidants.

- To prepare the dragon fruit, slice off the skin and cut the flesh into bite-sized pieces. If you can't get your hands on dragon fruit, use mango or another tropical fruit.

- The pavlovas can be made a day ahead and stored in an airtight container.

EDIBLE FLOWERS

I'm obsessed with edible flowers! I can't think of another ingredient
that achieves such spectacular impact with so very little effort. I think
it's because the flowers themselves are works of art, so they can't help but
add colour and beauty to every dish. Yet they also add flavour, nutrients
and in some cases medicinal benefits. Plus, there are just
so many ways to use them.

I happen to live close to an organic edible-flowers farm in Byron, and I've gained some useful tips from farmer Janelle.

USE EDIBLE FLOWERS TO:

› Decorate cakes and desserts, especially pavlova (see my Mini Matcha Pavlovas with Coconut Yoghurt and Fresh Fruits recipe on page 92).

› Transform a simple salad into a dish in its own right just by scattering flowers among the other ingredients.

› Create impressive garnishes in soups and breakfast dishes such as muesli, porridge and yoghurt.

› Freeze the flowers in ice cubes to add to drinks and cocktails – gorgeous!

› Sprinkle them in tea.

› Use them in baking for beautiful colour, flavour and fragrance. I love a hint of lavender in date scones.

COMMON EDIBLE FLOWERS

Some of the most common edible ornamental flowers include calendula, rose, sunflower, jasmine, lavender, elderflower, viola, pansy, chamomile, marigold, nasturtium, dianthus, freesia, stock and cornflower. Many herb flowers are edible and usually taste like the herb themselves. They include chives, garlic, leek, basil, rocket, borage, chervil, coriander, fennel, ginger, mint, oregano, rosemary, sage and thyme. Common edible vegetable flowers include broccoli, okra, radish and zucchini.

You can usually find edible flowers at farmers' markets or online. You can also try growing some among your herbs or create a beautiful floral array in a big pot. Most nurseries will have tubestock for varieties like chamomile and nasturtium which are very easy to grow.

PREPARING EDIBLE FLOWERS

› Wash gently by submerging the flowers in a bowl of water and then pat them dry with paper towel. Don't run them under the tap as this may damage the delicate petals.

› Store them in an airtight container in the fridge.

SAFETY

› If you suffer from hay fever or allergies to pollen, it's best to avoid them. Either way, edible flowers should be introduced gradually into your diet.

› Make sure you only use flowers that are edible as some can be poisonous. Although the internet is a good source of information, it's best to buy organic, packed flowers from shops and markets – if in doubt, leave it out.

› Don't eat flowers that are not organic, as they may contain pesticide residue.

NO-BAKE MACADAMIA
AND CHOCOLATE CHIP COOKIES

MAKES 12

Believe it or not, these are my dad's favourite cookies. I whipped them up one day at my parent's place, when I was craving a nutty choc-chip cookie but wanted it to be quick and healthy. As they're a 'no bake' cookie, I placed half of the batch in the fridge and the other half in the freezer to see which one would set better and have a nicer texture, only to find that most of the ones in the fridge had gone! Dad asked me if I'd baked the amazing treats in the fridge and said he was struggling to stop himself from eating the lot! Lucky they were wholesome. Even luckier I'd stored half the batch in the freezer, which upon sampling we both agreed tasted the best. Only problem is, I now have nowhere to hide them.

1 tablespoon linseeds, soaked
   in 3 tablespoons of water
   for 10 minutes
3 tablespoons almond butter
2 tablespoons coconut oil
2 tablespoons maple syrup
3 medjool dates, pitted
1 teaspoon vanilla powder
pinch of sea salt
90 g (1 cup) toasted rolled oats
35 g (¼ cup) roasted macadamia
   nuts, chopped
45 g (¼ cup) dark chocolate chips

Line a tray or plate with baking paper and set aside.

In a food processor, place the linseeds (and any soaking water), almond butter, coconut oil, maple syrup, dates, vanilla and sea salt in a food processor and pulse until it forms a smooth paste. Add the oats in three stages, pulsing in between until well combined. Add the macadamias and pulse briefly, so they're combined but still chunky. Add the chocolate chips and pulse to mix.

Roll tablespoonfuls of the dough into balls and arrange them on the prepared tray or plate. Press down on the balls with your palm or fingers until they resemble thick cookies. I like to make a crosshatch in the middle with a fork. Place in the freezer for 1 hour to chill and harden. Enjoy!

HOME-BREW KOMBUCHA

MAKES ABOUT 2 LITRES

I started making my own kombucha a few years ago, and I've now converted quite a few friends. The way it goes is this: my friends come to visit me, they ask what's in the crock, they're totally repulsed by the gooey scoby inside, but they give the kombucha a try anyway and end up asking for a lesson on how to make it! My besties recently nursed the jars of scobys I'd given them all the way home to Sydney – love it! Kombucha is basically a fermented sweet tea that's been consumed for centuries as a tonic for its many health benefits. It uses a scoby – the acronym for Symbiotic Culture Of Bacteria and Yeast (also called a 'mother') – which feeds off the sugar in the tea to produce a slightly effervescent and sour probiotic drink, a little bit like sparkling apple cider. Like other fermented foods, from sauerkraut to yoghurt, kombucha is purported to have gut-healing properties that help improve immune function, detoxify the body, support the nervous system and provide extra energy. You will need a kombucha crock, some glass bottles with screw tops or swing-top lids, muslin cloth and a large rubber band – oh, and a scoby. While you can buy your starter culture online, it's even better if a friend can give you a 'baby' scoby (you can literally peel off layers) and a little kombucha liquid to get your batch started.

1.5 litres (6 cups) unchlorinated water (see note)

220 g (1 cup) organic sugar

6–8 organic black or green tea bags

125 ml (½ cup) distilled white vinegar

250 ml (1 cup) kombucha starter liquid

1 scoby

Bring the water to the boil in a large saucepan, then stir in the sugar until it dissolves. Remove from the heat, add the tea bags and steep for about 10 minutes. Allow to cool completely. This can take a few hours, so if you want a faster way of cooling, make a more concentrated sweet tea from 1 litre (4 cups) water with the tea bags and sugar, then add 500 ml (2 cups) cold water after steeping.

Meanwhile, sterilise your crock with boiling water and rinse with the distilled white vinegar. (Don't use soap or dishwashing liquid, as you don't want any chemicals interacting with your kombucha.)

When the sweet tea is cold, add it to the kombucha crock along with the starter liquid and scoby. Place a square of muslin cloth over the top of the crock and secure with an elastic band. This allows the liquid to breathe but stops dust and bugs from getting in.

Leave it to ferment undisturbed somewhere warm (22–29°C) for about 2 weeks, and you'll have your own kombucha! During this time the scoby may sink to the bottom, start growing stringy bits and/or another film of scoby may form on top of your liquid. These are normal signs that your scoby is thriving. What you don't want is any mould (which will be green or black) or other strange growths. If you notice these, throw it out and start again.

Taste the kombucha after 1–2 weeks. If it's too sweet, allow it to ferment further; if it's too acidic, add some more cold sweetened tea according to the ratio in the recipe.

When your kombucha is ready, sterilise your glass bottles (run through a hot dishwasher cycle or boil for 10 minutes in a large pot on the stove) and allow to cool. Decant the kombucha into the bottles, leaving the scoby and 1 cup of kombucha in the crock.

Seal the bottles and store in the fridge to stop the fermentation process. If you want your kombucha a little carbonated, bottle it when it's still a little sweet, so that it ferments further in the bottle, but exercise extreme caution when opening the bottle, as you don't want it to explode – seriously, it can! If you like, you can flavour your kombucha when bottling. My favourite flavours are strawberries, ginger and herbs (see page 102).

Once you've consumed about two-thirds of your bottled kombucha, it's time to top up the crock with a new batch of sweet tea. This will give you another batch ready to go in a week or so. Your brew will eventually get so strong that you can top up and drink it as early as the next day, and you'll get into a rhythm where you just 'know' when it needs to be topped up and when it's ready. Once it has doubled or tripled in size, or has grown a 'baby', you'll be able to peel off some of your scoby to give to a friend.

NOTES

- Unchlorinated water is essential for the fermentation process, as chlorine can kill the good bacteria. For the same reason, make sure your kombucha only comes into contact with your crock and glass, not stainless steel or plastic, as it's an 'active' liquid.

- It can take your tummy a bit of time to get used to the extra burst of flora, so it's best to start off with a small dose in the morning (50–100 ml) and work up to three hits a day. It's especially refreshing with some ice and I like to add some sparkling water.

- Kombucha is a natural detoxifier, so drink plenty of water to help with the process.

STRAWBERRY AND GINGER KOMBUCHA 'MOJITO'

SERVES 4

While kombucha is a refreshing and healing drink in its own right, when combined with a few simple ingredients, such as rosemary, mint leaves and edible flowers, it also makes the perfect appetiser at a dinner party. I've never met anyone who doesn't like it! My favourite combination is strawberry and ginger, but feel free to experiment with your own flavours. For an alcoholic version, you can add 30 ml rum or vodka to each glass, though you may want to sweeten it with a little honey.

crushed ice
400 ml kombucha (see note)
600 ml soda or sparkling water
8 strawberries, sliced
8 thin slices of ginger
mint leaves, to serve
4 rosemary sprigs, to serve
edible flowers, to serve (optional)

This drink is the easiest thing ever to make! Divide crushed ice between four glasses. Pour 100 ml of kombucha into each glass and top up with 150 ml of soda or sparkling water. Divide the strawberries and ginger among the four glasses. Top each with mint leaves, a rosemary sprig and edible flowers. Enjoy!

NOTE

You can use store-bought kombucha or make your own version very easily and cheaply by using my recipe on page 100. You'll need to get it going at least 2 weeks before you plan to serve it.

FOOD FOR BABIES

I absolutely *love* cooking for my family, especially my son Archie.
I remember how excited Darren and I were about giving him solids for the
first time – there was so much discussion around what his very first 'taste'
would be. Sweet potato? Apple? Banana? In the end, pumpkin won. Classic,
earthy, warming, grounding with both sweet and savoury notes (sounds like
I'm describing a wine!), and perhaps best tasted in its simplest form,
or mashed with coconut oil or ghee.

It's been such a joy rediscovering foods and appreciating basic flavours all over again through Archie. I've been even more inspired to learn about the nutritional benefits of different foods in an effort to nourish him and provide him with strong foundations for a healthy mind and body. I want Archie to reach his full potential and good food is such a crucial beginning. We hope he shares our love of good food and grows to enjoy as many different flavours and cuisines as possible. More importantly, we want him to have a healthy relationship with food and to learn how to nourish himself. In our modern lives, so many traditional food preparation techniques have been lost in favour of faster food – even basic ones like making pancakes or boiling an egg. But Archie's been watching me cook in the kitchen since the day he was born, and I can't wait for him to join me; his little hands arranging veggies on a salad, patting scone dough, or holding a spoon covered in cake mix up to his delighted face!

My approach towards feeding Archie is the same as it is for myself and Darren – cooking with unprocessed, spray-free (wherever possible), seasonal wholefoods. *Real* food. So even with a hectic life, I prioritise making time to prepare fresh food. The trick is to make meals that we can all enjoy. We all quite happily ate porridge and fruity purees, such as banana and avocado mousse for breakfast, during his first few months of solids. We kept them simple for Archie, occasionally adding some yoghurt, nut butter and a little spice, while we'd top ours with crunchy nuts, cacao nibs and bee pollen. Baby purees are also great repurposed as dips, sauces and soups.

TO COOK OR NOT TO COOK?

While I cook the majority of Archie's meals fresh, preparing food in batches and freezing portions is a great option if you work or have many mouths to feed. Your homemade food will always be tastier and more nutritious than something from a packet or jar. In fact, it can be a good idea to have some backups in the freezer, especially on the difficult days. I'm fortunate that I love cooking, so for me, having to prepare fresh food was a calming circuit breaker in those first few months. And I've been making the most of it, as it might not be so calm once there's more than one child!

FIRST FOODS

While there are different viewpoints, most of the literature recommends starting your baby on solids at 4–6 months. This is because from around 6 months of age, babies require more than breastmilk to meet their nutritional needs, especially iron, vitamin D and protein. I started Archie at around 5 months with fresh, unprocessed, nutrient-rich wholefoods – something my paediatrician encouraged ('give him everything in the first year!'). Though I started off with simple, grounding foods that were gentle on his developing digestive system, they weren't necessarily bland in flavour. My trick was to make him food that I'd want to eat myself, so if he didn't want it, it wouldn't go to waste. And I'd offer Archie a particular food many times before I decided that he didn't like it. I figured that babies are no different to us: sometimes they just don't feel like something, aren't hungry, might be thirsty, not in the mood or simply don't recognise the texture.

Grounding fruits and vegetables

New fruits and vegetables can be introduced as quickly as you like – there's no need to do pumpkin for a week and then move on to the next thing. Having said that, I've eased him into various foods gradually, starting with the simplest, such as cooked and mashed root vegetables, apples and pears as well as banana and avocado, to give his little developing digestive system a chance to get used to all of these new foods. They can be served alone or mixed with a liquid like breastmilk, formula or boiled and cooled water.

Eggs and meat

These provide protein and the all-important mineral, iron. Egg yolk and liver are excellent sources of iron. I bought good-quality organic liver from the butcher, divided it into teaspoon or tablespoon-sized portions and froze it in zip-lock bags, so it was ready to go. I cooked the liver with Archie's steamed vegetables to make purees a couple of times a week. After a few weeks, I introduced poached chicken and fish, and after a few months a little red meat, too.

Good fats

I like to enrich meals with good fats, such as a teaspoon of coconut oil, ghee or bone broth. Pureed fruits are also delicious with a teaspoon of nut butter or a little spice like vanilla, cinnamon or nutmeg.

Wholegrains

When it comes to wholegrains, I try to soak them the night before with some lemon juice (about 1 teaspoon per cup of dried grain), to make them more digestible, and then cook as normal the next day. Mind you, I don't do this all the time, as I often forget or run out of time. Brown rice and quinoa are favourites, as Darren and I like to eat those, too. Oats are a breakfast staple because we all love them.

From around 9–12 months, I'd give Archie some sourdough bread to chew on occasionally. I don't have any issues with gluten but I prefer sourdough breads as they are slow-fermented with a starter which makes them more digestible.

Dairy

There are various schools of thought on the pros and cons of introducing dairy to infants, so it's always best to consult a trusted health practitioner. (I was fortunate to be able to see Dr Howard Chilton, a wonderful paediatrician and neonatologist who has a practice in Bangalow.) The main advantage of dairy is calcium, though calcium can also be found in decent quantities in almond nut milk, fish and vegetables. For example, 250 ml (1 cup) of cow's milk contains 300 mg of calcium while 85 g of sardines contains 371 g calcium. Because I was breastfeeding, the only dairy I gave Archie in the first year was ghee, and occasionally a little organic, plain, full-fat cultured yoghurt as a snack from about 8 months.

What about sugar?

Until Archie knows what sweets are, I've chosen to avoid refined sugar altogether and focus on just giving him fruit, but not fruit juice. The time will come when he discovers cakes and ice cream (hopefully homemade!), and I'm happy for him to enjoy them occasionally, as we do. Plus, I don't think I'll be able to control his grandma's urge to give him a treat! Ingredients like honey, raw and unrefined sugars, butter and flour make the most delicious sweets. I'm just not keen on artificial colours, additives, flavours and preservatives. I don't think of sweet foods as 'good' or 'bad' – they have a place in our family life – they are just considered 'sometimes' foods and usually based on whole, real ingredients. I still look back fondly to summer days on my grandma's farm in Poland, eating delicious strawberries with thick cream and a dusting of icing sugar and the Nutella sandwiches Dad used to make us.

SOME OF MY FAVOURITE FIRST-FOOD PUREES

I used to make a double portion of these to feed myself and Archie as they were so delicious!

Oat porridge with apple or pear, almond nut butter and cinnamon

Cook the oats according to the packet instructions, with either water or homemade almond milk (see page 47) and the fruit (cooking the fruit makes it gentler on the tummy). Let it steam for at least 5 minutes before pureeing with a teaspoon of nut butter and a pinch of cinnamon. (If I remembered, sometimes I soaked the oats the night before at a ratio of 2:1 water to oats, adding a couple of teaspoons plain yoghurt and popping it in the fridge. The next day, I cooked them in the soaking liquid, adding more water if necessary.)

Pumpkin, carrot and egg

Steam the pumpkin and carrot until soft, boil an egg and then puree together.

Sweet potato, pumpkin and coconut oil

Steam the sweet potato and pumpkin until soft, add a little coconut oil and puree.

Banana and avocado

This is a fantastic travel food as there's no cooking required. Simply carry the whole fruit with you, peeled and pitted, then mash it in a bowl. Archie had his plain, and I added crunchy nuts and bee pollen to mine.

Watermelon, papaya and yoghurt

Just blend and enjoy.

HUMID

COOLING AND EXOTIC FLAVOURS.
ASIAN DISHES, SEAFOOD, ICE-COLD DESSERTS.

Humid days conjure up floaty white cottons and kaftans with the murmur of ceiling fans. Falling asleep in a hammock under a canopy of palm trees. Lying by the pool drinking cold young coconuts. Afternoons spent watching monsoonal dark clouds gather, exploding into thunderstorms that squeeze the moisture out of the air. It's balmy nights, cocktails and the tropical aromas of chilli, ginger and lemongrass wafting from hawker street stalls. Barbecues, fresh seafood, citronella and frangipani trees. It's the reminiscence of a carefree childhood, dancing nude under sprinklers on seemingly never-ending summer days and being allowed to play outside until the sun sets. The song of the ice-cream van playing Greensleeves. Cooling rainforests and refreshing waterfalls. The body is perfectly nourished by fresh seafood and quenched by icy-cold pineapples, mangoes and popsicles.

PRAWN AND VEGETABLE ROLLS WITH MACADAMIA NUOC CHAM

MAKES 8

These Vietnamese-style prawn and vegetable rolls are a crunchy, punchy mouthful of nutritious yum and so refreshing in the warmer months. They're perfect for lunch, as well as a starter or canapé. If I'm entertaining, sometimes I like to serve them open to show the beautiful filling and have my guests 'roll their own'. I'm a big fan of kelp noodles for their iodine and other trace minerals, plus they happen to be fat and gluten free. The silverbeet leaf makes a perfect pouch for these rolls. It adds striking colour, is packed with vitamins and fibre, and less bitter than the more popular kale.

50 g kelp noodles (see note)

150 g cooked, peeled, deveined tiger prawns, cut into 1 cm pieces, tails removed

1 small carrot, cut into matchsticks

2 spring onions, thinly sliced

50 g snow peas, trimmed and cut into matchsticks

⅓ cup mint leaves, thinly shredded lengthways

⅓ cup coriander leaves

8 silverbeet leaves

Macadamia nuoc cham

1 small red chilli, finely chopped

1 tablespoon raw honey

2 tablespoons boiling water

1 tablespoon Thai fish sauce

1 tablespoon lime juice

2 tablespoons finely chopped salted roasted macadamia nuts

To make the nuoc cham, place all of the ingredients in a heatproof jug and stir until the honey dissolves. Set aside.

Place the kelp noodles in a large bowl and snip into 2 cm pieces. Add the remaining ingredients, then pour over half of the macadamia nuoc cham. Toss gently to combine.

Bring a large saucepan of water to the boil over high heat. Blanch the silverbeet, in batches, for 10–15 seconds then immediately drain and rinse under cold running water. Pat dry then remove the white stalks.

Arrange the leaves on a clean work surface with the stem ends facing towards you. Place ⅓ cup of the noodle mixture at the stem end of each silverbeet leaf. Fold each side over the mixture, then roll up tightly. Serve the rolls with the remaining macadamia nuoc cham for dipping.

NOTES

- If you can't find kelp noodles, substitute the same quantity of brown rice vermicelli or bean thread noodles. Just soak these in boiling water for 5–8 minutes or until they soften. Drain well, then snip into 2-cm pieces.

- You can also serve these as open-ended rolls by not folding in the sides of the silverbeet leaves before rolling.

RAW SNAPPER WITH FENNEL, PICKLED BEETROOT AND BUTTERMILK DRESSING

SERVES 6

There's something elegant and effortless about a beautiful plate of raw fish, especially on a hot summer's day when the last thing you want to do is slave away at a stove. You'll need to start this recipe the day ahead to pickle the beets, but it's oh so worth it, and once that's done it literally takes just minutes to put together. Ask your fishmonger for the freshest sashimi grade fillet available, and then rejoice at the fact that you don't have to cook it!

400 g sashimi-grade
    snapper fillet
1 Lebanese cucumber,
    thinly sliced
1 baby fennel, thinly sliced,
    fronds reserved
1 green apple, cored and cut
    into matchsticks
edible flowers, to serve (optional)

Pickled golden beetroot

100 ml white wine vinegar
50 g sugar
1 star anise
60 g (about 3) golden baby
    beets, scrubbed and thinly
    sliced, leaves reserved
    (optional)

Buttermilk dressing

160 ml (⅔ cup) buttermilk (for
    a recipe see note on page 236)
zest and juice of 1 lime
4–5 cm piece of ginger,
    finely grated
sea salt and freshly ground
    black pepper
splash of pickle juice from
    the pickled beetroots

To prepare the pickled beetroot, place the vinegar, sugar and star anise in a small saucepan with 100 ml of water and bring to the boil. Remove from the heat and allow to cool. Add the beetroot, cover and leave to pickle for a good 24 hours in the fridge.

To make the dressing, combine the ingredients in a small jug and mix well.

Slice the snapper into 4-mm thick slices and arrange on a plate with the cucumber, fennel, apple and beetroot. Drizzle over the dressing and garnish with the fennel fronds and beetroot leaves, and edible flowers, if using.

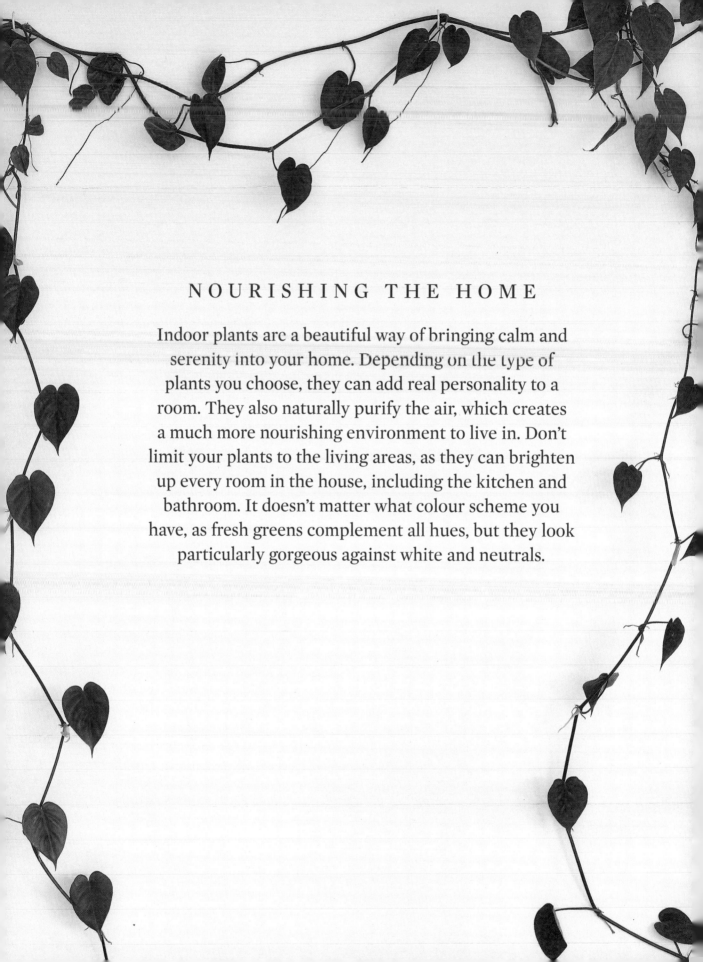

NOURISHING THE HOME

Indoor plants are a beautiful way of bringing calm and serenity into your home. Depending on the type of plants you choose, they can add real personality to a room. They also naturally purify the air, which creates a much more nourishing environment to live in. Don't limit your plants to the living areas, as they can brighten up every room in the house, including the kitchen and bathroom. It doesn't matter what colour scheme you have, as fresh greens complement all hues, but they look particularly gorgeous against white and neutrals.

I don't have much time to take care of plants, so all of my favourites happen to be low maintenance!

Fiddle-leaf fig (*Ficus lyrata*)

If you have a beautiful pot, this is the plant to save it for, as it has a wow factor. It's large, sculptural and very on trend, working especially well in living areas where it will command the attention it deserves. It's a tropical plant, so it thrives best in filtered light, warmth and humidity. Water when the top layer of soil gets dry, around once a week, and give the leaves a wipe occasionally (plants 'breathe' through their leaves).

Zanzibar gem (*Zamioculcas zamiifolia*)

Darren once called this plant elegant, and that's exactly what it is! We've had it in our bathroom for years, and I'm really not sure if anyone waters it but it stands proud, tall and green. It's virtually indestructible!

Swiss cheese plant (*Monstera deliciosa*)

I love the beautiful, big leaves of this gorgeous plant and the lush tropical feel it adds to a space. It's actually the same plant that bears the delicious 'fruit salad' fruit, which looks like a cob of corn but tastes just like a tropical fruit salad. This is a tropical plant that likes warmth, filtered light and moisture. Water when the top layer is dry and occasionally wipe the leaves.

Cacti (*Cactaceae*)

Their reputation for requiring very little care is well known, and I love the boho desert feel that cacti add to the home. A few pots of cacti clustered together in different pots look great. Just keep them out of reach of little hands!

String-of-pearls (*Senecio rowleyanus*)

This delicate plant looks beautiful on a shelf or hanging in a macramé basket where its pea-like tendrils can cascade down. Pop it in a bright, sunny spot, give it a good water and then let it dry out a bit between watering. Do note, however, that it's best to have it hanging up high away from pets and children, as it is considered to be toxic.

Devil's ivy (*Epipremnum aureum*)

I love this climber as it's so versatile and low maintenance. You can let the lush leaves drape down, or if they're long they are a work of art when pinned up against a wall. Keep the leaves out of reach of pets and children, as they are poisonous. Allow the top soil to dry out between watering.

Spider plant or 'airplane' plant (*Chlorophytum comosum*)

It looks so impressive with its dangling 'spiderettes', yet this is one of the easiest indoor plants to keep alive. All it needs is bright, filtered light, well-drained soil and the occasional watering. You can plant any spider 'babies' in their own pots by placing them in soil while still attached to the mother plant. Water them well, and once their own roots form you can cut them from the mother plant.

GREEN GODDESS GAZPACHO WITH
TURMERIC CREAM AND DUKKAH

SERVES 6

It doesn't need to be winter for you to enjoy a nourishing bowl of soup. In fact, this beautiful green version of the traditional, cold gazpacho is incredibly refreshing on a humid day and the ultimate glow food. It has the goodness you'd expect from a super-duper green juice, yet there's the added creaminess from the avocado and turmeric cream, plus a bit of crunch and spice from the dukkah. As there is no cooking involved, it not only takes just minutes to prepare but also retains every bit of nutrition. When food is chilled it loses some of its flavour, so don't be shy with the chillies, garlic and ginger – you'll want them!

1 small head of iceberg lettuce, cored and roughly chopped (trimmed weight 450 g)

200 g baby spinach leaves

2 Lebanese cucumbers, roughly chopped

3 garlic cloves, peeled

2 long green chillies, trimmed and roughly chopped

3 cm piece of ginger, peeled

1 bunch of flat-leaf parsley, roughly chopped

1 cup mint leaves, plus extra to serve

750 ml (2½ cups) cold vegetable stock

2 chilled avocados

60 ml (¼ cup) lemon juice

sea salt and freshly ground black pepper

olive or avocado oil, to drizzle

1 tablespoon dukkah (see note)

handful of edible flowers (optional)

Turmeric cream

125 ml (½ cup) double cream or Greek yoghurt

3 teaspoons grated turmeric (see note)

Working in three batches using a high-powered blender, blend the lettuce, spinach, cucumber, garlic, chilli, ginger, parsley, mint and stock until very smooth. Strain through a fine mesh sieve into a large jug, using the back of a spoon to press out as much liquid as possible. Cover the jug and chill for 1 hour. Reserve the pulp for another use (see note).

Meanwhile, place the cream and turmeric in a small bowl and stir gently until combined. Cover and chill until required.

Return the chilled gazpacho to a clean blender jug. Add the avocado and lemon juice and blend until smooth. (You need to blend the avocado just before serving as it oxidises when left to rest.) Season to taste. Serve with a drizzle of oil and a sprinkle each of dukkah, mint leaves and edible flowers, if using. Finish with the turmeric cream – I like to swirl it through the gazpacho.

NOTES

• Don't throw away the pulp! You can freeze it and then thaw and use it in your green smoothies or add it to a soup or casserole dish.

• Dukkah is an Egyptian condiment made from ground mixed nuts, seeds and spices. It's widely available in delis and supermarkets.

• If you can't find any fresh turmeric, simply use 1½ teaspoons ground turmeric.

BROCCOLI SLAW

SERVES 4

This is the perfect salad for a picnic or barbecue on a hot day. It's crisp, fresh and bursting with flavour. I've added 'buckinis' (activated buckwheat kernels), which are full of protein and have a great crunchy texture, but broccoli is the hero – and rightfully so, it actually contains more vitamin C than oranges! This slaw makes a substantial meal on its own, but is also a great accompaniment to chicken and fish.

500 g broccoli, florets shredded, stems cut into matchsticks

150 g white cabbage, finely shredded

2 apples, cored and cut into matchsticks

2 spring onions, thinly sliced

100 g (½ cup) buckinis (see note)

40 g (¼ cup) roasted almonds, chopped

flat-leaf parsley and mint leaves, to serve

Dressing

250 ml (1 cup) buttermilk (for a recipe see note on page 236)

1 tablespoon apple cider vinegar

1 tablespoon white chia seeds

1 tablespoon honey

1 teaspoon dijon mustard

To make the dressing, combine all of the ingredients in a jar, secure the lid and shake well. Allow to sit for 30 minutes (longer if possible) for the chia seeds to gel.

Place the broccoli, cabbage, apple, spring onion and buckinis in a large bowl. Pour over the dressing and toss well. Season to taste and top with the almonds, parsley and mint.

NOTE

Buckinis are soaked and dried ('activated') buckwheat kernels and can be found in health-food stores. Good substitutes include toasted sesame, sunflower or pumpkin seeds.

SOBA NOODLE SALAD WITH WAKAME
AND MISO-POACHED CHICKEN

SERVES 4

This Japanese-inspired dish brings back lovely memories of our old home in North Bondi, where we'd have a soba noodle salad every week during summer. It's light, fresh and perfect for a midsummer lunch or dinner on a balmy night. The wakame seaweed is one of the ultimate glow foods with its high doses of magnesium, iodine, calcium and vitamins. I love the miso-poached chicken for its flavour and tenderness, but you can also try this salad with an oily fish, such as salmon or trout. Trust me – you will feel great after eating this!

2 tablespoons white miso paste

20 g dried wakame, soaked in cold water for 10 minutes, then drained

2 spring onions, roughly chopped, plus extra, thinly sliced, to serve

4 cm piece of ginger, sliced

500 g chicken breast fillets

180 g soba noodles

2 teaspoons sesame oil

250 g daikon, cut into matchsticks (see note)

160 g (1 cup) frozen podded edamame beans, blanched

1 Lebanese cucumber, trimmed, halved lengthways and thinly sliced

90 g (⅓ cup) pickled ginger

1 teaspoon black sesame seeds

shredded nori sheet, to serve

Dressing

180 g (¾ cup) sour cream

2 spring onions, finely chopped

1 tablespoon rice wine vinegar

2 teaspoons soy sauce

1 teaspoon sesame oil

Place the miso, wakame, spring onion, ginger, chicken and 500 ml (2 cups) of water in a saucepan over high heat. Bring to a simmer then reduce the heat to low, cover with the lid and gently poach for 10–12 minutes until the chicken is cooked. Remove from the heat and allow the chicken to sit in the poaching liquid for 20 minutes before removing from the pan and slicing thickly. Strain the poaching liquid, reserving the wakame for the salad and 125 ml (½ cup) of the liquid for the noodles. Discard the spring onion and ginger.

Cook the noodles in a saucepan of boiling salted water for 3–4 minutes. Drain the noodles under cold running water and transfer to a bowl. Pour over the reserved strained poaching liquid and sesame oil, and mix to combine. Cover and refrigerate until required.

To make the dressing, whisk the ingredients in a bowl until well combined.

To serve, toss the noodles with the reserved wakame, daikon, edamame and cucumber, and transfer to a serving platter. Top with the chicken, extra spring onion, pickled ginger, sesame seeds and nori, and drizzle over the dressing.

NOTES

- If you want to make pickled daikon, pour 250 ml (1 cup) of water into a small saucepan with 80 ml (⅓ cup) rice wine vinegar, 1 tablespoon sugar, 1 tablespoon mirin and 2 teaspoons sea salt. Cook over low heat for 1–2 minutes or until the sugar has dissolved. Pour the liquid over the daikon, and set aside for 20 minutes to cool.

- The pickled daikon, chicken and noodles can all be made a few hours in advance – just cover and refrigerate until needed. If you prepare the noodles in advance, pour an extra 125 ml (½ cup) of strained chicken poaching liquid over them, as they will soak up the liquid.

ONE-PAN WHOLE-BAKED SNAPPER

SERVES 2–3

I came up with this dish when Mum brought over a beautiful whole snapper, and I needed to make do with whatever was in the fridge. But as Darren would say, that's when the magic happens! Luckily, I'd been to the farmers' market a couple of days before, so I had some fennel, tomatoes, olives and capers knocking around. The beauty of this dish is that it takes about 15 minutes to prepare the sauce, using only one pan, then you pour yourself a vino and put your feet up while the oven does the rest. Even if you happen to leave it in the oven for a little too long, it still stays nice and moist due to the sauce and steaming. It's hearty and filling on its own, but it's delicious with white rice or farro, too. If you want to stick to the one-pan rule then begin the recipe now and leave the capers in the sauce. But if you're willing to bend the rules a little by using an extra pan (it's only a small one!), then you can take this dish to the next level by topping it with crispy, fried capers – your choice, but I know what I'd do!

1 tablespoon ghee

1 garlic clove, crushed

1 onion, diced

1 fennel bulb, thinly sliced

2 tomatoes, roughly chopped

40 g (¼ cup) olives, pitted and
    roughly chopped

2 tablespoons capers, drained
    and rinsed (see note)

sea salt and freshly ground
    black pepper

250 ml (1 cup) dry white wine

1 lemon

1 x 600 g whole snapper, cleaned
    and gutted

small handful of torn flat-leaf
    parsley leaves, to serve

small handful of dill fronds,
    to serve

Preheat the oven to 200°C.

Heat the ghee in a large ovenproof frying pan over medium heat. Sauté the garlic, onion and fennel for about 10 minutes, until soft. Stir in the tomato, olives and capers (if you're not frying them), season to taste and cook for about 2 minutes until the tomato starts to fall apart and create a sauce. Pour in the white wine and cook the mixture for another couple of minutes until the wine has reduced and the sauce smells divine.

Meanwhile, zest the lemon, then cut it in half and slice one of the halves into semi-circles. Set the remaining half aside.

Score the fish 3–4 times diagonally on both sides, making the incisions on one side large enough to fit the slices of lemon.

Remove the pan from the heat and place the fish on top of the sauce, spooning some of the mixture over the fish and into the cavities. Push the lemon slices into the scored incisions. If the fish is too big for the pan, cut off the tail or head and put it back in the pan – don't throw it away! Cover the pan with foil and place it in the oven to cook for about 15–20 minutes or until the internal temperature of the fish reaches 60°C (you can check this with a meat thermometer). If you're cooking a larger snapper (say 1 kg), it will take around 25–30 minutes. Remove from the oven, discard the foil and squeeze the remaining lemon over the fish. Serve, topped with the lemon zest, torn parsley and dill. Season with sea salt and pepper and serve immediately.

NOTE

To make crunchy capers, omit the capers from the sauce then, while the fish is baking, toss the capers in 1 tablespoon of cornflour and fry in a small frying pan in 1 teaspoon of ghee over medium heat until crisp and golden brown. Scatter over the top of the fish when ready to serve.

NATIVE FOODS

When I think of Byron Bay, I instantly think of buttery macadamias, zingy finger limes, tart Davidson plums and zesty lemon myrtle. But what about the other 5000 or so native Australian food species? My work as a meteorologist has given me an intense appreciation of Australia's diverse climate and how it has impacted the development of our unique native plants, many of which have had to really fight to survive, making them not only incredibly resilient but also very high in nutrients. The crazy thing is, many of us are more familiar with exotic varieties like acai and goji berries than the rainforest edibles and bush foods growing right under our noses. Take for instance the Kakadu plum, grown in our Top End. It's the richest known source of vitamin C in the world. Yup, more than oranges – plus it is higher in antioxidants than the more widely known blueberry.

Not only are we fortunate to have our very own supercharged rainforest and bush foods right here in our own backyard, but native crops are more suited to thrive in Australia's harsh climatic conditions (making them more sustainable), and they're absolutely delicious! So why don't we see more of them in our food industry? I think a lot of it comes down to supply chains. Some of these amazing foods can be a little tricky to find, as they only grow in the wild. However, macadamia farmers have been incredibly successful in farming this native nut commercially, especially here in Byron Bay, and there could certainly be more focus on doing this with other foods like finger limes and Davidson plums. But importantly, this needs to be achieved by collaborating with local indigenous communities who, as the original custodians of this country, offer thousands of years of skills and knowledge. This is particularly important for wild, poisonous and elusive varieties of desert and rainforest foods that can't necessarily be scaled to meet market demands; and to ensure that we only take what we need. Perhaps it will force us to eat truly seasonally according to Australia's unique climate, rather than the concept of four seasons borrowed from the northern hemisphere. *This* is sourcing locally and being truly sustainable. What an opportunity!

Here are some of my favourite native foods:

Lemon myrtle (*Backhousia citriodora*)

The leaves of this tree have a lovely citrus scent and taste a lot like lemongrass. They're high in antioxidants, calcium, zinc, magnesium and vitamin E and are delightful in tea and for flavouring fish and desserts.

Riberry (*Syzygium luehmannii*)

Also known as a small leaved lilly pilly, the bright berries have a spicy bush chai flavour with notes of clove and cinnamon. They're lovely in jams, with meats such as lamb, as well as in salads and desserts. They're particularly high in folate, which is important during pregnancy.

Atherton raspberry (*Rubus probus*)

This dense shrub produces gorgeous bright red raspberries that taste milder than European varieties, but are delicious nonetheless – just be careful to avoid the spiky stems!

Finger lime (*Citrus australasica*)

This stunning 'zesty caviar' is my all-time favourite citrus fruit and comes in many different flavours and colours. It's high in vitamins C and E and potassium, and is delicious with all seafood (oysters are my favourite), desserts and spirits.

Wattleseed (*Acacia*)

There are close to one thousand acacia species in Australia, but only a few produce edible seeds – the rest are toxic. The most commonly harvested include the mulga (*A. aneura*), golden (*A. pycnantha*) and silver wattle (*A. retinodes*). When roasted and ground, the seeds have a nutty flavour a little like coffee and chocolate, so they're lovely added to desserts like my Sweet Potato and Wattleseed Chocolate Brownies (see page 240). The seeds are high in magnesium, iron and fibre.

Macadamia nuts (*Macadamia*)

Creamy, buttery, crunchy macadamias are high in thiamine (B1), which is important for metabolising carbohydrates, and the minerals manganese and magnesium. I love them in cereal and desserts, but they also make a great nut milk and fish crumb.

Kakadu plum (*Terminalia ferdinandiana*)

This fruit contains the highest recorded levels of vitamin C in the world and is a rich source of antioxidant compounds. Commonly used in jams, it is great in sauces and desserts. I have used it in dehydrated powder form in water (like vitamin C powder) to treat colds.

Davidson plum (*Davidsonia*)

This native plum has both sweet and savoury notes, a bit like a tart beetroot. High in potassium, magnesium and manganese, it is great in jams and preserves.

Tasmanian pepperberry (*Tasmannia lanceolata*)

Also known as mountain pepper, this tastes like pepper but with much more heat! It's high in calcium, zinc, magnesium, manganese and antioxidants, and can be used in soups, casseroles, pasta and stews, but in smaller amounts.

BYRON BIBIMBAP

SERVES 4

Bibimbap was one of our 'family meals' for years, but not one that we ever cooked ourselves. I grew up in Sydney in a suburb known as Korea Town, and as a weekly treat Mum and Dad would take me and my sister out for Korean food. Despite the amazing selection of dishes, my go-to has always been dolsot bibimbap with a side of kimchi. It's a tradition I now continue with Darren every time we visit my parents, and hopefully one Archie will enjoy, too! Dolsot bibimbap is traditionally eaten from a very hot, heavy pottery bowl, which crisps up the rice and cooks the raw egg yolk when you stir it through, but in the absence of a dolsot bowl at home I make it with a fried egg, and it tastes just as authentic.

400 g rump steak or 200 g
    tempeh, cut into thin strips
1 garlic clove, crushed
1 tablespoon soy sauce
1 tablespoon sesame oil
pinch of brown or rapadura sugar
pinch of sea salt and freshly
    ground black pepper
400 g (2 cups) brown rice
1 tablespoon of sesame or
    grapeseed oil
100 g shiitake mushrooms, sliced
1 spring onion, finely chopped
250 g spinach, roots trimmed,
    leaves and stems roughly
    chopped
1 teaspoon sesame seeds, toasted
2 small carrots, cut into
    matchsticks
splash of olive oil
4 eggs
80 g (1 cup) bean sprouts
kimchi, to serve

Sauce
2 tablespoons gochujang or
    chilli paste
1 tablespoon sesame oil
1 tablespoon apple cider vinegar
½ garlic clove, crushed
1 tablespoon sesame seeds,
    toasted

Place the steak or tempeh in a bowl with the garlic, soy, sesame oil, sugar, salt and pepper and toss to evenly coat. It will smell divine! Pop it in the fridge to marinate for 30 minutes or so.

Meanwhile, place the brown rice and 875 ml (3½ cups) of water in a saucepan and bring to the boil. Reduce the heat to low and simmer, covered, for 20–25 minutes or until most of the liquid has been absorbed. Remove from the heat and leave to steam for another 10 minutes with the lid on. Set aside, but keep warm.

Heat the sesame or grapeseed oil in a non-stick frying pan over medium–high heat and cook the marinated steak 5 minutes (the tempeh for 2–3 minutes), or until browned on all sides. Remove from the pan, cover and keep warm.

Using the same pan over medium heat, fry the mushrooms for 1–2 minutes in the beef or tempeh juices until soft and fragrant. Set aside.

Now pop the spring onion in the pan and fry for 1–2 minutes until just starting to brown. Add the spinach and cook for about 1 minute until wilted. Stir through the sesame seeds, then remove from the pan and set aside.

If there is any juice left in the pan, pour most of it out onto the steak or tempeh. (This prevents the carrot from colouring.) Return the pan to the heat and fry the carrot for 1–2 minutes or until it begins to soften. Remove from the pan and set aside.

Place the sauce ingredients in a small jug and mix well.

Return the pan to medium heat and add a splash of olive oil. Fry the eggs until the whites are set and the yolks are runny.

Divide the brown rice among four bowls and arrange the meat/tempeh, carrot, mushrooms, spinach and bean sprouts in little mounds around the inside edge of the bowls, leaving some space in the middle for the egg. Pour over the sauce (or serve it in individual dishes so people can help themselves) and sit the egg on top. To eat in the traditional way, stir the sauce and ingredients together so the egg breaks up and it looks a bit like fried rice. Enjoy with a side of kimchi.

MACADAMIA- AND COCONUT-CRUMBED FISH WITH RAINBOW SLAW

SERVES 4

You've spent the day at the beach. You are sun-kissed and hungry but want something light yet satisfying. This is the meal for you! It's based on one of my favourite childhood dishes: crispy fish and coleslaw. Mum and Dad would regularly take my sister and I on road trips up the coast and the holiday officially started when we'd get to the local chipper. This recipe is perfect for a barbecue or lazy weekend dinner, and packs a major flavour and nutrition punch! While it wasn't my intention, it also happens to be gluten, sugar and dairy free.

60 g (½ cup) goji berries
200 g red cabbage, shredded
1 cup chopped kale, stems
   removed
¼ red onion, thinly sliced
1 carrot, cut into matchsticks
1 cucumber, cut into matchsticks
1 tablespoon roughly chopped
   mint leaves, plus extra to serve
1 tablespoon roughly chopped
   coriander leaves, plus extra
   to serve
120 g (1 cup) macadamia nuts,
   chopped
2 tablespoons chopped flat-leaf
   parsley leaves
10 g (⅛ cup) shredded coconut
50 g (½ cup) coconut flour
3 eggs, lightly beaten
4 (about 600 g) skinless white
   fish fillets
2 tablespoons coconut oil
lemon wedges, to serve

Dressing
1 avocado
140 g (½ cup) tahini
1 garlic clove, chopped
2 tablespoons apple cider vinegar
juice of 1 lime
sea salt and freshly ground
   black pepper

First, rehydrate the goji berries by placing them in a small bowl and covering with water. Leave to soak for 10–15 minutes until they plump up. Drain, reserving the juice for the dressing.

Place the red cabbage, kale, red onion, carrot, cucumber, mint, coriander and goji berries in a large salad bowl and toss with your hands.

To make the dressing, place the avocado, tahini, garlic, vinegar and lime juice in a food processor and blitz until creamy. Gradually add the goji berry soaking water (up to ½ cup) until the dressing reaches the desired consistency. Season with salt and pepper and mix through the slaw.

Now it's time for the fish. Place the macadamia nuts in a food processor and blitz until they form a rough crumb. Tip them into a bowl and stir through the parsley and coconut. Place the coconut flour in another bowl and the beaten egg in a third. Dip each fish fillet in the flour, then in the egg and finally coat in the macadamia mixture.

Melt the coconut oil in a frying pan over medium heat and cook the fish for 1–2 minutes on each side or until golden brown and crisp. Serve with the rainbow slaw, lemon wedges and extra coriander and mint leaves sprinkled over the top.

COCONUT RICE NOODLES WITH PRAWNS, GREEN MANGO AND FRESH COCONUT

SERVES 4–6

Coconut, mango and prawns – that's summer right there. For me, nothing beats drinking a fresh young coconut on a hot and sticky day. Not only do I recommend drinking one while you make this dish, but you can also use the fresh coconut flesh inside as your garnish. Prawns are a treat, and I always make sure that what I'm buying is Australian and sustainably caught (ask your fishmonger about this when you purchase them). Otherwise, you can substitute local, line-caught fish or even tofu. You can eat these noodles hot or cold, but when it's humid I always go for the latter.

150 g flat rice noodles

1 green mango, thinly sliced
    into matchsticks

2 spring onions, thinly sliced

150 g mixed red and yellow
    cherry tomatoes

350 g snake beans, cut diagonally
    into 5 cm lengths

160 g bean sprouts

1 long red chilli, sliced (see note)

600 g cooked, peeled, deveined
    king prawns (tails intact)

½ bunch of coriander, leaves
    picked (see note)

40 g fresh coconut shavings

4 kaffir lime leaves, finely
    shredded

2 tablespoons finely chopped
    unsalted peanuts

2 tablespoons fried shallots

lime wedges, to serve

Dressing

2 tablespoons fish sauce

2 tablespoons lime juice

2 tablespoons coconut milk

2 tablespoons grated palm sugar
    (see note)

2 cm piece of ginger, finely grated

1 lemongrass stalk, white part
    only, finely grated

1 garlic clove, crushed

To make the dressing, place all of the ingredients in a glass jar with a lid and shake well. Set aside until needed.

Place the noodles in a large bowl and pour over boiling water to cover. Allow to soak for 3–4 minutes, then drain and return to the bowl. Set aside for 15 minutes to cool. Add the mango, spring onion, tomatoes, beans, bean sprouts and chilli.

Just before serving, pour over the dressing, toss to combine and transfer to a serving platter. Top with the prawns, coriander, coconut, shredded lime leaves, peanuts and fried shallots. Serve with lime wedges on the side for squeezing over.

NOTES

- Adjust the amount of chilli to your liking – long red chillies are cayenne chillies, which are not as hot as bird's eye, so if you like it hot, add more!

- Reserve the coriander roots and stems for the Mullum curry recipe on page 184.

- Palm sugar is a mineral-rich sweetener made from the nectar of coconut palm flowers or the sap of various palm species (including coconut and date palms). It involves minimal processing and happens to be low GI, too. It can be purchased from Asian grocers in solid blocks or granulated form and can be dark or light coloured, depending on the source.

ALMOND MILK PANNA COTTA WITH FRESH FRUITS AND CHAI HONEY SYRUP

SERVES 4

This little dessert is much easier than it looks and is a great one to make the night before. There are so many delicious flavours coming together with the almond, vanilla, cream and exotic chai spices. It makes a nutritious and refreshing breakfast during summer, too, though you might want to hold the amaretto!

olive oil, for greasing
1 vanilla pod (see note)
250 ml (1 cup) sweetened almond milk (see note)
250 ml (1 cup) pouring cream
1 tablespoon honey
2 gelatine leaves
fresh fruits of your choice (e.g mixed berries or figs when they are in season)
edible flowers, for garnish (optional)

Chai–honey syrup

1 teaspoon tea leaves
2 cm piece of ginger, sliced
1 cinnamon stick
6 cardamom pods, bruised
6 black peppercorns
3 cloves
2 tablespoons honey
2 tablespoons amaretto

Lightly oil four ½-cup capacity ramekins or panna cotta moulds.

Using a small, sharp knife, split the vanilla pod lengthways and gently scrape the insides to remove the seeds. Place the seeds in a small saucepan with the almond milk, cream and honey. Bring to a gentle simmer over medium heat.

Meanwhile, soak the gelatine leaves in cold water for 5–10 minutes or until just softened. Squeeze out the excess liquid and add the gelatine to the cream mixture, stirring for 1–2 minutes until dissolved. Strain the cream through a fine sieve into a jug, then pour into the prepared ramekins or moulds. Cover and refrigerate for 2–3 hours or until set.

For the syrup, pour 500 ml (2 cups) of water into a small saucepan. Add the tea, ginger, cinnamon, cardamom, peppercorns and cloves and bring to the boil. Reduce the heat to low and simmer for 2–3 minutes. Remove from the heat and set aside for 15 minutes to infuse.

Strain the liquid through a fine sieve and discard the solids. Return the liquid to the pan, add the honey and amaretto and bring to a gentle simmer over medium heat. Cook for 3–4 minutes or until slightly thickened and syrupy. Pour into a jug and set aside until needed.

To serve the panna cotta, carefully run a thin bladed knife around the insides of the moulds and invert onto serving plates. Top with the fresh fruits, a drizzle of syrup and edible flowers, if using.

NOTES

- Never throw a vanilla pod away! Use it to make your own vanilla extract instead. Put the pod in a tall, narrow jar and pour alcohol (such as vodka) over it until it's fully covered. Leave to infuse for a couple of months in a cool, dark place. Alternatively, you can bury it in a jar of caster sugar to make beautiful vanilla-scented sugar.

- To make your own sweetened almond milk, soak 250 g raw, unsalted almonds in filtered water overnight. Drain. Place the almonds, 4 pitted medjool dates and 1 litre (4 cups) fresh filtered water in a food processor and blitz until smooth. Strain through muslin. It will keep in the fridge for 2–3 days. Spread the leftover almond solids onto a tray, dehydrate in the oven and use as almond meal in baking.

COOKIES AND CREAM

MAKES 7

My biggest guilty pleasure is cookies-and-cream ice cream. I just love it! This is my nutritious take on it – a malty vanilla 'nice cream' sandwiched between two fudgy chocolate cookies. It's very easy to make and incredibly tasty. These look really gorgeous arranged in a stack on a plate, and your friends will be surprised when they realise they're not 'Oreos' but ice cream sandwiches, and even more surprised when they learn they're vegan. If you're after a quick treat, the nice cream is pretty amazing on its own and takes just 2 minutes to make. The maca powder has its origins in Peru and has been used medicinally for thousands of years. The benefits include balancing hormones and fighting stress and fatigue, but I love the malty taste it adds to the nice cream.

120 g spelt flour

30 g cacao powder

80 g coconut sugar

¼ teaspoon bicarbonate of soda

sea salt

1 teaspoon vanilla powder

45 g coconut oil, melted

45 ml almond milk (for a recipe see page 47)

50 g chopped dark chocolate or cacao nibs

'Nice cream' filling

1 frozen banana, thawed for 10 minutes (see note on opposite page)

2 teaspoons almond butter

2½ tablespoons almond milk

½ teaspoon vanilla powder

1 teaspoon maca powder

To make the cookies, mix the dry ingredients in a bowl. Place the coconut oil, milk and chocolate or cacao nibs in a food processor and pulse until well combined. Add the dry ingredients and pulse until they form a dough. Place the dough on a clean work surface and shape into a ball. Cover with plastic wrap and refrigerate for 30–60 minutes to firm up.

Preheat the oven to 150°C and line a baking tray with baking paper.

Roll the dough out to a thickness of about 5 mm. Cut 14 cookies with a 6 cm round cookie cutter and place them on the prepared tray. Bake for 12–15 minutes. Transfer to a wire rack to cool completely – they should be fudgy yet a little crisp.

To make the nice cream filling, place all of the ingredients in a food processor and pulse until smooth and creamy.

To assemble the cookies, scoop 1 tablespoon of nice cream onto the centre of a cookie and top with another. Press down gently until the cream reaches the edges and then use a palette knife or small spatula to smooth the sides. Pop the cookies in the freezer as you go, then freeze them all for at least 2 hours. To serve, allow to stand at room temperature for a few minutes before tucking in. (This is so they soften a little and your friends can admire your efforts before the cookies disappear!)

CHOCOLATE MOUSSE WITH COCONUT AND BERRIES

SERVES 4

It's hard to believe that this rich, creamy and chocolaty mousse is refined sugar free, vegan and made from banana and avocado! It's delicious on its own or served with frozen berries and shaved coconut. There's no cooking or setting, so it takes just minutes to whip up – a totally doable weekday snack or dessert.

1 frozen banana, thawed for
    10 minutes (see note)
1 avocado
25 g (¼ cup) cacao powder
3 tablespoons maple syrup
½ teaspoon vanilla extract
pinch of sea salt

To serve
mixed frozen berries
shaved coconut

Place all of the mousse ingredients in a food processor with 3 tablespoons of water and pulse until smooth and creamy. Place in four serving glasses and chill for at least 1 hour before serving. Top each with a quarter of the frozen berries and shaved coconut.

NOTE

The frozen banana is the secret to the ice cream-like consistency. I like to keep sliced bananas handy in zip-lock bags in the freezer, so they're easy to break apart for smoothies, snacks and desserts.

MAKE YOUR OWN HAIR GARLAND

Hair garlands are such a fresh, feminine and effortless way to look and feel beautiful on a special occasion. Whether you're a bride or mum to be, a birthday girl or a boho goddess, you'll love having flowers in your hair. They suit every celebration from whimsical weddings to country picnics. The lovely Elle from Flowers at The Farm in Byron Bay first taught me how to make one for my baby shower, and together we made the perfect, polished flower crown. Why not gather your girlfriends together to make garlands over wine and cheese (or tea and cakes).

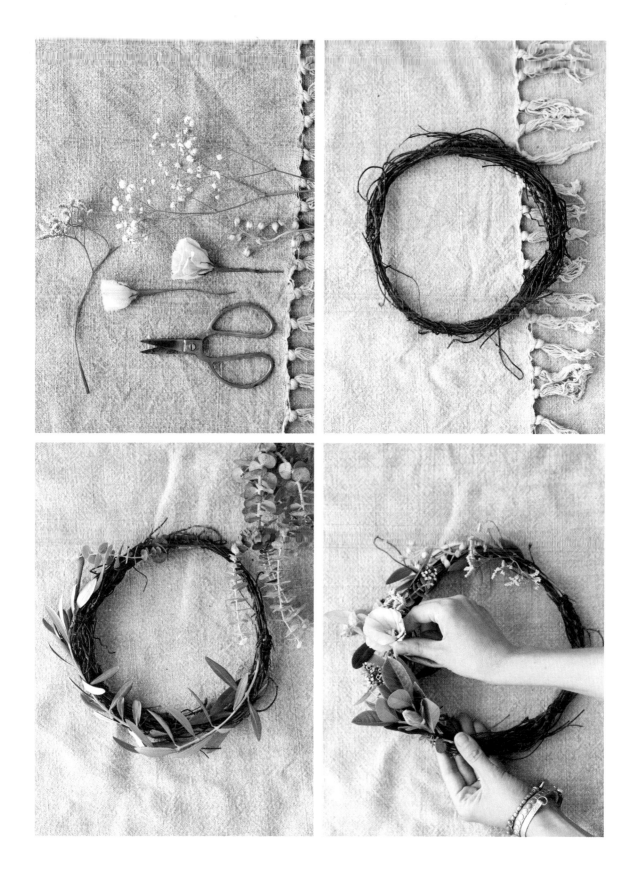

If you're a bride on a budget, a hair garland is the perfect accessory, as you can make one for under $30. It's worth getting the right floristry materials (they're available from most craft stores), as they make the garland look very professional.

Materials

› dodder vine
› 12 green floristry wires (6 thin and 6 medium)
› scissors
› floristry tape
› green, spriggy foliage, such as jasmine, eucalypt
  or any variety of *Thryptomene*
› fresh seasonal blooms

Pull away a nice semi-thick strand of brown dodder vine. Shape the dodder vine into a circle and intertwine to join at the back. Wrap a few lengths of thin floristry wire around the garland to lightly secure. Snip off any strays with your scissors. Now that you have your base, you're halfway done.

Cut some strands of the green jasmine and thread them through the dodder vine, securing with a little piece of thin wire if need be. Repeat with the eucalyptus, thryptomene or whatever spriggy foliage you have, until you have a light covering all the way around.

Now it's time to wire up your blooms. Take one length of medium floristry wire and gently push it through the top of one stem (just under the petals) until 1 cm is poking through. Carefully bend both sides of the wire downwards so they run parallel to the stem. Cut the flower stem nice and short. Starting from the top, wrap the floristry tape tightly around the stem and wire all the way to the bottom. (It helps if you stretch the tape a little as you wrap, so it's tight.) This step is awesome as it makes the whole garland look polished, and your blooms last longer as you're sealing the stem with the tape. Repeat for the remaining blooms.

Now attach your flowers to the garland. It's best to start with the biggest bloom – put it at the front or just off-centre, and then arrange the other blooms around it. Insert the covered stems into the dodder vine and either wind the stems around the vine, or secure with a small piece of wire if necessary. It doesn't need to be perfect. It's all about making a relaxed boho-style crown. I hope you love it!

POPSICLES, THREE WAYS

Frozen popsicles are loved by both grown-ups and kids and make the best refreshing snack on hot summer afternoons. These are nutritious enough to have for breakfast and gorgeous enough to serve as a dessert at a dinner party or barbecue. Since they're made the night before to allow for freezing time, it's the kind of dessert you can just whip out on the day with a gin and tonic in hand. So effortless! I like to arrange mine on a bed of ice with some torn mint, which pairs so well with fruit. Once you've made them, feel free to experiment with your favourite types of fruit and herbs. Assembling them is so much fun, and it's satisfying when you take them out of the mould and see all the beautiful colours blending into each other.

BLUEBERRY FIELDS

MAKES 8

This popsicle is inspired by the deliciously sweet blueberries I get from the farmers' market each week. They're grown in Brooklet, a short drive away, so they're always fresh. Blueberries can be a little tart, especially after freezing, so I like to sweeten them with honey. These are great for breakfast on the run!

300 g (2 cups) blueberries, fresh or thawed

2 tablespoons honey

55 g (¼ cup) caster sugar or honey (see note on opposite page)

1 teaspoon vanilla extract

420 g (1½ cups) Greek yoghurt

Gently mix the blueberries, honey and 2 tablespoons of water in a bowl or jug and set aside.

Place 125 ml (½ cup) of water in a saucepan with the sugar or honey and bring to the boil over a medium heat. Reduce the heat and simmer for 5 minutes or until the sugar has dissolved (or the honey is pourable). Set aside to cool. (This syrup not only gently sweetens the yoghurt but also gives it the right consistency for pouring into the moulds.)

Use a stick blender to blend the blueberry mixture for a few seconds until it is just starting to look mushy but still has blueberry bits through it (you don't want to liquefy it).

Place the vanilla and yoghurt in a bowl or jug and mix well. Slowly stir in the cooled syrup until you achieve a nice, smooth, pouring consistency.

Now the fun part! Assemble the popsicles by pouring the blueberry and yoghurt mixtures into popsicle moulds in alternate layers, leaving 1 cm free at the top of each mould. Try to pour the blueberry mixture so it touches the sides of the mould as this is how you get that gorgeous mottled look.

Place the moulds in the freezer for about 2 hours before gently inserting wooden sticks into the partially frozen popsicles. Continue freezing for another 2 hours or overnight.

COCONUT CREAM, WATERMELON AND PISTACHIO CRUMB

MAKES 12

This amazing flavour combination reminds me of Turkish delight, and tastes so decadent that it's great for a dinner party. Consider using the rosewater as it transforms it into something special.

2½ cups cubed watermelon
(to make 400 ml puree)
½ teaspoon rosewater (optional)
1 x 400 ml can coconut cream
2 tablespoons honey (see note)
70 g (½ cup) shelled pistachios,
chopped

Place the watermelon and rosewater, if using, in a blender and pulse to a smooth puree. Pour the mixture into 12 popsicle moulds until each is about one-third full. Freeze for about 2 hours. (This layer needs to be at least partially frozen before adding the coconut layer.)

In a jug, whisk together the coconut cream and honey then pour it over the frozen watermelon layers until it's about 1 cm from the top of each mould. Return to the freezer for 2 hours or until just starting to set. Remove from the freezer, sprinkle over the chopped pistachios, pressing them in lightly if necessary. Insert wooden sticks and continue to freeze for at least another 2 hours or overnight.

BYRON SUMMER

MAKES 8

There's something so exciting about the first harvest of mangoes in summer, and they are definitely the hero of this popsicle. I like to add some chopped strawberries, kiwi fruit, passionfruit and basil for extra colour and flavour.

1 mango, cubed
4 strawberries, hulled and halved
1 kiwi fruit, peeled, halved
lengthways and sliced into
8 semi-circles
1 tablespoon chopped basil leaves
2 tablespoons passionfruit pulp
500 ml (2 cups) coconut water

Assemble your popsicles by alternately placing a piece of mango, strawberry and kiwi fruit into 8 popsicle moulds, with a little basil and passionfruit pulp between each piece. Pour in the coconut water until the liquid is about 1 cm from the top of the mould. Place the moulds in the freezer. After a couple of hours, insert wooden sticks into the partially frozen mixture. Return to the freezer for at least another 2 hours, preferably overnight.

NOTES

- To remove popsicles from their moulds, place them in a container of warm water for about 20 seconds until they loosen. This kicks off the melting process, so if you want them to stay frozen for longer when serving to guests, my tip is to take them out of their moulds a few hours before, pop them in a zip-lock bag and return them to the freezer.

- The sweeteners in all of these recipes are optional, but it's worth noting that the ingredients aren't as sweet when they're frozen, so you can go a little sweeter than normal.

- If you're using honey as your sweetener, it's important to use a light-coloured, plain honey, so it doesn't overpower the other flavours.

Coconut cream, watermelon
and pistachio crumb

Blueberry fields

Byron summer

SERVES 6

Humid weather always takes me back to holidays in places like Bali and Thailand making me crave tropical fruits and Asian flavours, such as pineapple, coconut, chilli, peanuts and kaffir lime. This dessert is perfect on a hot, balmy night, after you've spent most of the day in the sun and surf and feasted on barbecued fish. John Picone, here in Byron Bay, grows the best pineapples I've ever tasted, including exotic red ones! If you don't have fresh pineapple to hand, other summer fruits such as watermelon, mango and passionfruit also work beautifully.

200 g (¾ cup) palm sugar, grated

1 lemongrass stalk, white part only

6 cm piece of ginger, sliced

2 kaffir lime leaves, torn, plus extra finely shredded to serve

2 small red chillies, split lengthways

2 large ripe pineapples, peeled, cored and roughly chopped

60 ml (¼ cup) lime juice

350 g coconut yoghurt

2 tablespoons toasted and roughly chopped unsalted peanuts

2 tablespoons toasted coconut flakes

Place the sugar, lemongrass, half the ginger, the lime leaves, chilli and 250 ml (1 cup) of water in a small saucepan over high heat. Stir for 2–3 minutes until the sugar dissolves. Continue to simmer for 1–2 minutes until syrupy. Remove from the heat and set aside for 30 minutes to cool and allow the flavours to infuse.

Place the pineapple and remaining ginger in an electric juicer to extract 750 ml (3 cups) of juice.

Strain the syrup into a large jug, discarding the solids, then add the lime and pineapple juice and stir. Pour into a shallow metal tray and freeze for 2 hours or until the mixture is partially frozen around the edges. Use a fork to drag ice crystals towards the centre of the tray then return the tray to the freezer for another hour. Repeat this process every hour another three or four times. It's ready when the ice crystals flake easily when scraped with a fork and are like a gritty sorbet.

Spoon the coconut yoghurt into serving glasses. Top with the granita, shredded lime leaves, peanuts and coconut flakes.

NOTE

If you don't like the idea of the chilli, feel free to omit it from the recipe – the ginger and lime provide plenty of zing.

THE CUBAN

MAKES 1

I was shown how to make this drink in the hottest and most humid place I've ever visited: Cuba. I'd been horse riding through the rich, green tobacco plantations of Viñales when our local guide decided to stop for a break. A group of us sat in a little shed while he proceeded to roll his own cigars in silence, with us *gringos* looking on in awe. From an esky, he pulled out icy-cold coconuts and cracked them open, to which he added a swig of local rum, some honey and a squeeze of lime juice. In that moment, with beads of sweat running down my face, it was the best drink I'd ever had. I can't think of a more refreshing, hydrating and nourishing beverage on a hot day. I decided to call it The Cuban.

1 fresh, young coconut, icy cold

30 ml (1½ tablespoons) Havana Club rum

2 teaspoons honey, or to taste

juice of ½ lime

To open your coconut, use a chef's knife to cut the husk or outer skin off the top. You do this by working your way around the top with firm cuts (a bit like gradually taking the tip off a boiled egg), until you reach the shell. Hit the coconut shell with the knife blade at a 45 degree angle and then use the incision to pry it open with the knife.

Pour the rum into the coconut followed by a drizzle of honey and the lime juice, then give it a quick stir. For maximum impact, it's best enjoyed while listening to Buena Vista Social Club.

'NATURAL' WINE

I first got hooked on natural wine during a trip to Europe. Darren and I were enjoying some of the great bars and restaurants in Paris, and I was surprised to discover that natural wines were favoured at many of them. Indeed, Paris turned out to be the heartbeat of the natural wine movement.

At first I found natural wines quite strange and a little 'funky', but they were refreshingly nuanced, interesting and subtle. More than that, I loved that sometimes I didn't know what I was going to get. This is partly because there's no *official* definition for what constitutes 'natural wine' – the basic idea is that they're wines that have been produced with as little human or technological intervention as possible. For this reason, they're traditionally made in small quantities by artisan or independent producers, using organic or biodynamic grapes that are hand-picked to protect soil biodiversity. No sugar, artificial yeasts or enzymes are used in production (the natural yeast present on the grape skin is used instead) and very little (if any) sulphur is used. Oh, and the wines are usually unfiltered. With these sorts of practices you can imagine that they're not made in huge quantities, yet they are still affordable. Some producers go a step further and rely on nature alone for irrigation, so if there's no rain the vines aren't watered.

Natural wines, therefore, aren't manipulated to suit the tastes of consumers, improve shelf life or maintain consistency. But this also means that natural wines can be inconsistent, have 'wilder' flavours and appear cloudy. As such, there's a lot of debate about whether these wines are 'inherently faulty'. In my experience, one in ten or twenty (yep, I like a glass of vino) may taste a bit off or funny, but I'm more than happy to take the gamble.

In an age of mass production, natural wines appeal to my appreciation for artisanal goods. I want to support smaller producers where possible, and I also feel better mentally and physically about drinking a wine free from additives, chemicals, herbicides and commercial yeasts. Natural wines are literally more 'alive', since the microbes and organisms that give the wines their unique character haven't been filtered out or killed off.

I still enjoy drinking conventional wines, but I'm finding myself gravitating more and more towards natural wines because I really like the unique flavours, the respect for nature and the wonderful stories behind them. One of my favourite local producers is a guy called Jared Dixon who owns Jilly Wines. If you're in the area, you can pay him a visit at his little wine cellar in Clunes.

CLOUDY

COMFORT FOOD FOR COZY DAYS.
SOUPS, STEWS, SLOW COOKS, CRUMBLES.

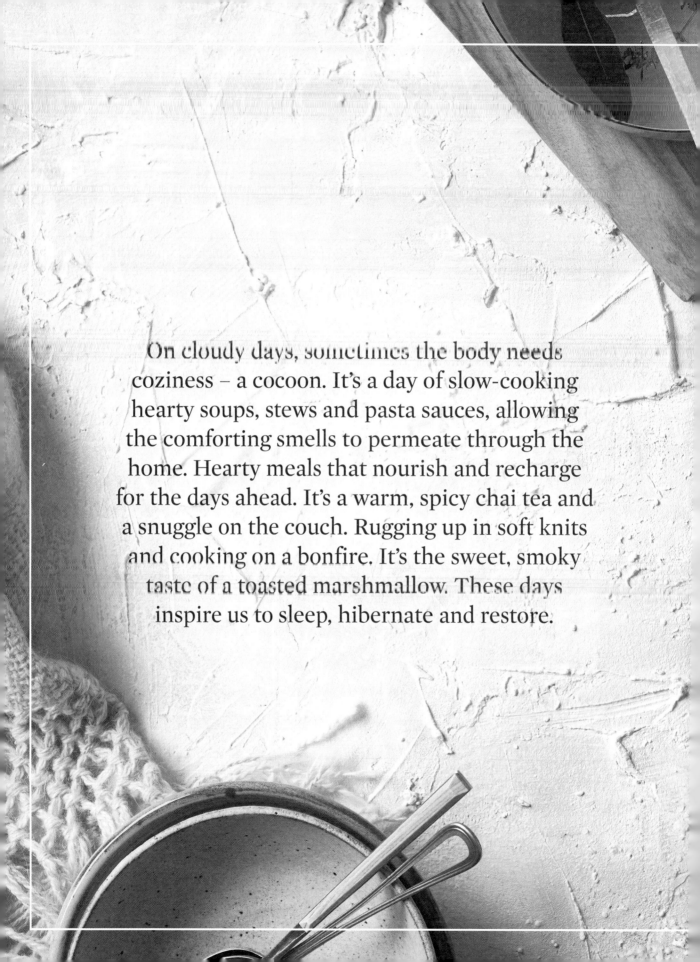

On cloudy days, sometimes the body needs coziness – a cocoon. It's a day of slow-cooking hearty soups, stews and pasta sauces, allowing the comforting smells to permeate through the home. Hearty meals that nourish and recharge for the days ahead. It's a warm, spicy chai tea and a snuggle on the couch. Rugging up in soft knits and cooking on a bonfire. It's the sweet, smoky taste of a toasted marshmallow. These days inspire us to sleep, hibernate and restore.

SLOW-ROASTED TOMATO AND TURMERIC SOUP

SERVES 6

I invented this recipe after buying some beautiful Coopers Shoot tomatoes at our local farmers' market and harvesting a heap of turmeric in our garden. At the time, Darren, Archie and I had all come down with colds, so I needed to nourish us with immune-boosting meals that were easy to make. And so the slow-roasted tomato and turmeric soup was born. It's packed with vitamin C and anti-inflammatory and antioxidant properties, plus it's just so delicious it's become a family favourite. It's funny how some of the best recipes are born out of necessity and a bit of creativity with leftovers. You don't need to worry too much about quantities in this one either. You really can't get it wrong.

2 kg tomatoes, roughly chopped

1 zucchini, roughly chopped

1 red capsicum, deseeded and roughly chopped

400 g pumpkin, deseeded and roughly chopped

5 garlic cloves, left whole

3 cm piece of ginger, roughly chopped

3 cm piece of turmeric, roughly chopped

1 rosemary sprig

5 basil sprigs, leaves and stems separated

60 ml (¼ cup) olive oil

sea salt and freshly ground black pepper

750 ml (3 cups) chicken or vegetable stock

crème fraîche or Greek yoghurt, to serve (optional)

Preheat the oven to 120°C.

Place the vegetables in a roasting tin. Add the garlic, ginger, turmeric, rosemary and basil stems. (Keep the leaves for serving – they don't do well in the oven and are much better fresh!) Drizzle over the olive oil and season with salt and pepper.

Place the tray in the oven, uncovered, and slow-roast the veggies, tossing occasionally, for 2–3 hours – the house will smell amazing!

Transfer the roasted veggies and any liquid from the tray into a large saucepan or stockpot, and use a stick blender to puree the mixture. Add the stock 250 ml (1 cup) at a time, until the soup reaches your desired consistency. Place over medium heat and bring to the boil. Remove from the heat and serve in bowls with the basil leaves sprinkled over the top.

Because the soup is made with fresh tomatoes and no sugar it has a slightly acidic taste. If you prefer it milder, serve it with a dollop of crème fraîche or Greek yoghurt. I've had mine with sourdough and cultured butter, too. The acidity mellows out with a little time, so it's even better the next day.

SLOW-COOKED LAMB RAGU WITH PAPPARDELLE

SERVES 6 PLUS LEFTOVERS

I *love* pasta and so does my bestie Jeanine. We eat out a lot together and love to try new dishes, but if there's slow-cooked ragu with pappardelle on the menu, forget about it, nothing else will get a look in! When I make this at home, I cook an extra lamb shoulder to use for another meal – that way, I make the most of the oven being on for such a long time. It only takes about 30 minutes to prepare, with the rest of the magic being in the slow cooking. As if slow-cooked lamb ragu wasn't enough, I've added wild forest mushrooms and a drizzle of truffle oil to give it a rich, earthy depth of flavour. I particularly like making this pasta on a cloudy day and enjoying it with a bottle red and great friends. If you're entertaining, you can make the ragu a day ahead, as the flavour will only improve with time. This one's for you, Jeanine!

50 g mixed dried forest
    mushrooms (see note)

2 tablespoons olive oil

1 onion, sliced

1 leek, white part only,
    thinly sliced

2 carrots, finely diced

2 celery stalks, finely diced

4 garlic cloves, roughly chopped

2 x 1.5 kg lamb shoulders, bone in

250 ml (1 cup) red wine

2 tablespoons tomato paste

4 large truss tomatoes,
    finely chopped

2 rosemary sprigs, leaves picked
    and chopped

4 thyme sprigs

2 fresh bay leaves

250 ml (1 cup) passata

500 g pappardelle, dried or
    homemade (for a recipe
    see page 183)

To serve

flat-leaf parsley leaves

shaved parmesan

truffle oil

Pour 250 ml (1 cup) of boiling water over the mushrooms and set aside for 1 hour. When rehydrated, remove the mushrooms from the soaking liquid and finely chop. Reserve 125 ml (½ cup) of the liquid.

Preheat the oven to 160°C. Heat half of the oil in a large heavy-based, ovenproof saucepan or flame-proof casserole dish over medium heat. Add the onion, leek, carrot, celery and garlic and cook, stirring, for 6–7 minutes until softened.

Meanwhile, heat the remaining oil in a large frying pan over high heat. Add the lamb and brown on all sides for 2–3 minutes. Remove the lamb, then deglaze the pan with the wine and add to the vegetables (see note on page 216 about deglazing). Stir in the tomato paste, tomato, rosemary, thyme, bay leaves, mushrooms and reserved mushroom liquid. Sit the lamb on top of the vegetables. Cover tightly with a lid or aluminium foil. Transfer to the oven and cook for 5 hours until the meat is falling off the bone. Check after 4 hours and add 125 ml (½ cup) of water if the sauce is reducing too much.

Remove the lamb from the oven and, using two forks, carefully shred the meat from the bone. Stir the meat through the sauce and add the passata. Discard the bones, bay leaves and thyme sprigs.

Increase the oven temperature to 180°C. Return the pan to the oven (uncovered) and cook for a further 45 minutes until the sauce is thick.

Meanwhile, cook the pasta in a saucepan of rapidly boiling salted water until al dente. Drain and transfer to serving bowls. Top with the ragu, parsley leaves, parmesan and a drizzle of truffle oil. Heaven! Pour yourself a glass of your favourite wine and enjoy.

NOTES

- You can find dried forest mushrooms in most gourmet grocers and delis. Otherwise, if you're like my mum and dad, you can go foraging for them yourself in autumn and dry them, so you have them all year round!

- If you're not using a heavy-based cast-iron pan you will need to reduce the cooking liquid by 1 cup.

ROASTED BONE MARROW WITH SOURDOUGH AND GREEN SALAD

SERVES 4

Bone marrow has got to be one of my favourite foods ever. Not only is it incredibly tasty, but it's also one of the most restorative and nourishing foods you can eat. I'd always thought it was the stuff of restaurants and chefs, but it's actually super easy and one of the cheapest meals you can make. If you're entertaining, it makes a great starter and is a definite crowd pleaser. Bone marrow is best served simply with toasted sourdough or focaccia and a small side salad.

2 tablespoons olive oil

2 garlic cloves, crushed

1 tablespoon finely chopped flat-leaf parsley leaves

4 beef marrow bones, cut in half lengthways (get your butcher to do this)

1 tablespoon lemon zest

sea salt and freshly ground black pepper

4 slices of sourdough, toasted

Green salad

large handful of mixed salad leaves

½ cup flat-leaf parsley leaves, roughly chopped

1 tablespoon capers, drained and rinsed

1 spring onion, sliced

2 tablespoons olive oil

1 tablespoon lemon juice

sea salt and freshly ground black pepper

Preheat the oven to 220°C and line a baking tray with baking paper.

Mix together the olive oil, garlic and parsley in a small bowl.

Arrange the bones on the prepared tray and brush the marrow generously with the olive oil mixture. Sprinkle over the lemon zest and season with salt and pepper. Place in the oven and roast for about 20 minutes or until the marrow is gooey but not melted.

Meanwhile, to make the salad, combine the salad leaves, parsley, capers and spring onion in a bowl and dress with the olive oil, lemon juice and salt and pepper, to taste.

To serve, use a knife to scoop out the marrow and spread it over the crusty sourdough. Pour any baking tray juices over the top, and place a portion of salad on the side. Use your bread to soak up every last morsel and enjoy!

SPELT PASTA SALAD WITH PESTO, GOAT'S CHEESE AND CHARRED BALSAMIC PEACHES

SERVES 4

This salad is inspired by the beautiful multi-coloured Coopers Shoot heirloom tomatoes that I buy from my local farmers' market. Tomatoes, basil and cheese would have to be one of my all-time favourite flavour combinations, and the tangy sweetness of the balsamic peaches takes it to another level. It's a great dish to take to a picnic, and I guarantee you'll come home with a clean bowl!

250 g spelt pasta spirals (fusilli)

60 ml (¼ cup) balsamic vinegar

1 tablespoon honey

2 large, ripe peaches, stones removed, cut into 8 wedges

1 tablespoon olive oil

260 g (1 cup) Kale, basil and roasted hazelnut pesto (see page 217), or store-bought pesto

160 g heirloom cherry tomatoes, halved (see note)

2 small zucchini, sliced into ribbons (see note)

150 g goat's feta, crumbled

¼ cup basil leaves, torn

sea salt and freshly ground black pepper

Cook the pasta according to the packet instructions until al dente.

Place the balsamic vinegar and honey in a small bowl and stir until combined. Add the peach wedges and gently toss until evenly coated.

Heat the oil on a chargrill pan over medium heat. Add the peach wedges and grill for about 2 minutes on each side until charred. Set aside.

When the pasta is ready, drain and stir through the pesto until evenly coated. Toss through the cherry tomatoes and zucchini ribbons and sprinkle the crumbled feta on top. Add the peach, scatter over the basil leaves and season with salt and pepper to taste. Enjoy immediately or refrigerate until you're ready to serve.

NOTES

- I love heirloom tomatoes because they come in so many beautiful colours, but of course, red ones are just as delicious!

- I slice my zucchini with a vegetable peeler but you can also use a mandoline.

DARREN'S SLOW-COOKED PORK WITH LEMON LEAVES, CLOVES, GINGER AND HONEY

SERVES 6 HUNGRY PEOPLE

It's hard to choose a signature dish for Darren because it's what the bloke does for a living, but if I were pushed I'd have to say it's his slow-cooked pork. It will change your life. Think perfectly sweet, smoky, spicy, fall-off-the-bone meat with the crispiest crackling ever. Now you might think that a big hunk of pork is an intimidating thing to cook properly, but it really only takes 15 minutes to prepare and the rest of the work is done in the oven. The magic is in the spices and technique. Some nights, I even take the whole pot with me down to the beach and reheat it over a bonfire. (I take the cooked crackling in a jar so it stays crunchy!) I love it with a Christmassy red wine like the Jilly Field Blend by my mate Jared at Jilly Wines in Clunes or, as Daz would say, a cheeky beer. You're welcome.

1 x 3 kg pork shoulder
1 tablespoon grapeseed oil
sea salt

Marinade

3–4 cm piece of ginger,
    thinly sliced
6 lemon leaves, torn
4 kaffir lime leaves, torn
2 garlic cloves, crushed
1 long red chilli, halved
4 tablespoons grapeseed oil
1 tablespoon smoked paprika
1 tablespoon coriander seeds
1 star anise
1 teaspoon cloves
1 tablespoon fennel seeds
sea salt and freshly ground
    black pepper
2 tablespoons honey

Preheat the oven to 200°C.

Remove the skin from the shoulder, score the top, and set aside in the fridge.

In a small bowl, combine all of the marinade ingredients except the honey. Place the pork in a baking dish or casserole dish and smother with the marinade. Roast, uncovered, for 10–12 minutes until the marinade becomes fragrant. Remove from the oven and add 250 ml (1 cup) of water to the bottom of the dish. Reduce the heat to 160°C, cover, and slowly cook for around 6 hours, checking after 4–5 hours. If the meat is not yet cooked, but there is not much liquid at the bottom, add a little more water. When the meat comes away from the bone, it's ready. Remove the dish from the oven and increase the heat to 200°C.

To make crackling, transfer the skin to a baking tray. Brush the skin with oil, liberally season with salt and roast for 20 minutes.

Meanwhile, add the honey to the juices at the bottom of the baking dish and use the mixture to baste the pork. Return it to the oven, uncovered, for 10 minutes to colour up, basting regularly. Remove from the oven and leave to rest while the crackling crisps up nicely.

Season the pork with a little more salt, smash up the crackling, throw it over the top and you're done! The pork is rich, sweet and succulent, so is best served with a crunchy, citrusy salad.

GET CREATIVE
WITH LEFTOVERS

I can't bear wasting quality food, especially when
it's been ethically grown and lovingly prepared.
Fortunately, there are so many excellent uses for the
offcuts and by-products of food preparation.
If all else fails, add vegetable scraps to your compost
and nourish the soil that feeds the food that nourishes
us! (My guide to composting is on page 205.) Here's
a list of my best tips for using leftovers.

Vegetable stalks and leaves

My favourite use for these is in a homemade pesto or salsa verde. You'd be surprised that even the most bitter leaves and stalks taste amazing with a bit of garlic, salt and olive oil. Pesto and salsa verde are great condiments to have in the fridge, as they transform even the blandest of meals into something tasty. Try my Carrot and Radish Leaf Salsa Verde on page 72, or use whatever stalks and leaves you have to hand instead of the kale in my pesto on page 217.

The stalks from herbs, such as rosemary, parsley and thyme, are great for flavouring soups, stews and ricotta, as they can be easily removed once cooked. Vegetable leaves and tops (such as carrot, celery and beets) are also great for soups, stews, or even juices.

Juice pulp

I use vegetable pulp to thicken sauces, stews and soups, or add to flour to make pizza dough. Sweeter pulps, such as apple, carrot and beetroot, make delicious additions to cakes and brownies.

Citrus peels

They're a perfect addition to drinks. Use them fresh as a zesty flavour in teas, water and cocktails. Or steep them in your favourite liquor, such as vodka, for a few days to make your own infused beverage. Darren also uses our dried peels for kindling.

Whey

I love using whey as a stock in risotto (see my Risotto with Peas and Homemade Ricotta recipe on page 86). It's also lovely in pancakes and muffins, and a good base for salad dressings. It's an ideal acid to add to water when soaking grains and pulses. You can even add a tablespoon to homemade pesto or hummus to help them last longer.

Egg whites

Egg whites are a key ingredient in marshmallows and meringues, and are a fantastic 'binder' in biscuits and nut bars. For something savoury, make an omelette, add them to stir-fries or use them to clarify your stock. (You strain your stock, return it to the pan and mix the egg white through. As it cooks, the egg white forms a 'raft' that any leftover small particles stick to, making the stock crystal clear.)

Egg yolks

These nuggets of nutrition should never, ever be wasted! They're essential in custards and curds, as well as creamy sauces like mayonnaise (see my Special Mayonnaise on page 70), béarnaise, hollandaise and carbonara. You can drop them raw into a soup or smoothie or stir-fry them with vegetables and rice.

Bread

Stale bread is perfect for making croutons or Panzanella salad (see page 64). If you know you're not going to use a whole loaf within a couple of days, slice and freeze some of it to use for toast or blitz in a food processor to make breadcrumbs.

Potato skins

These make gorgeous, crunchy potato chips! Preheat the oven to 200°C and line a baking tray with baking paper. Give the skins a wash and soak them in warm water for about 15 minutes. Pat dry and place on the baking tray. Drizzle over some olive oil, season with sea salt, freshly ground black pepper and a smattering of your favourite herbs, and bake for about 30 minutes, until golden and crunchy. Allow to cool for a few minutes and enjoy them on their own or tossed through salads.

Rice and grains

Whenever a recipe calls for rice, quinoa or other grains I always cook extra, as having them on hand makes it very easy to whip up a meal. I often make a quick special-fried rice for breakfast or lunch by frying some brown rice with eggs, peas and any other leftover veggies in a little coconut oil with soy sauce and lemon juice. Cooked grains also make a lovely porridge when heated up with some milk, cinnamon, honey and fruit.

Leftover roast meat and veggies

Leftover beef, lamb, chicken and veggies make the *best* fillings for one-pot pies, salads, wraps, frittatas, omelettes, burritos, quiches... the list is endless!

Chicken, beef and fish bones

Use these to make nourishing stocks and healing broths (see my Healing Chicken Broth on page 212).

MUM'S CABBAGE ROLLS

MAKES 12–14

I grew up eating Polish food, which sounds great now but wasn't cool at the time. I used to have salami, mustard and gherkins on rye bread for my school lunches, and all I wanted was to have meat pies and sausage rolls like the other kids. I appreciate it now, though! These *gołąbki* or stuffed cabbage rolls were my favourite dinner, and it's still a real treat when Mum makes them. They're soooooo good! Like most Polish dishes, every mum and grandma (*babcia*) does them her own way, and of course I think my mum's are the best! She's passed down her special recipe, and now you can enjoy this comforting, cloudy-day recipe, too. Trust me, you'll be making this one time and time again.

1 white cabbage

200 g (1 cup) long-grain white rice

500 g pork mince

2 white onions, diced

4 garlic cloves, crushed

2 tablespoons chopped flat-leaf parsley leaves

sea salt and freshly ground black pepper

2 x 400 g cans diced tomatoes

5 button mushrooms, sliced

1 tablespoon cornflour mixed with 125 ml (½ cup) water

2 bay leaves

10 whole black peppercorns

¼ teaspoon allspice berries (see note)

125 ml (½ cup) chicken stock or water

Remove the stem of the cabbage by cutting around the bottom. Place the cabbage in a large stockpot, stem side down, and cover with salted water. Bring to the boil and simmer for 15 minutes. Using tongs or a fork, carefully remove the first layer of 3–4 cabbage leaves and place them on a tray to cool. Continue cooking the cabbage for 5 minutes then remove the next layer of 2–3 cabbage leaves. Do this every 5 minutes until you have 14 leaves.

Meanwhile, cook the rice in 500 ml (2 cups) of salted boiling water for 10–15 minutes until the liquid has been absorbed. Set aside to cool. Once cool, (it can still be a little warm), place it in a bowl with the pork and half each of the onion, garlic and parsley. Season with salt and pepper and mix well. (Mum always combines the ingredients with her hands, as it's gentler on the rice.)

Take a cabbage leaf and slice off the thick membrane on the underside. Place it flat on your work surface with the stem closest to you. Take about a palm's worth of the pork and rice mixture and place it in the centre of the leaf, 3 cm from the bottom. Fold this 3 cm 'flap' up and over the mixture, then fold over the sides and roll it up. Repeat with the remaining leaves and mixture.

Peel 6 more leaves from the cabbage and place 3 of them in the bottom of a large saucepan. Stack the cabbage rolls on top of the leaves and set aside.

In a large bowl, mix together the tomatoes, mushrooms, cornflour mixture, bay leaves, peppercorns and allspice. Add the remaining onion, garlic and parsley and stir until well combined. Season with salt and pepper. Now pour the sauce over the top of the cabbage rolls and if it doesn't cover them, add chicken stock or water until they are just covered. Place the remaining 3 cabbage leaves on top to seal and cover the pot with a lid. Cook on medium heat until boiling, then reduce to a simmer and cook for 2 hours.

To serve, place the cabbage rolls in shallow serving bowls and top with a ladle of sauce. They are best enjoyed with boiled potatoes and a gherkin.

NOTE

Allspice berries (also called pimento or Jamaican pepper) are a sweet and aromatic spice with hints of clove, cinnamon and nutmeg. If you can't get the berries, use ground allspice.

LAMB SHANKS WITH SWEET POTATO MASH

SERVES 4

Lamb shanks are just the perfect winter food. They're warming, comforting, wholesome and so tasty. Because they're slow-cooked, they also create the most gorgeous aroma in the house. It immediately makes me want to put on my trackies, pour a glass of red and make guests feel at ease. I love this as a family meal, as it saves me from having to make something separate for the baby. The ghee provides a good dose of nutritious fat and the hint of nutmeg is a nice way to introduce spices to a developing palate. I like to serve this dish in shallow bowls to scoop up the delicious sauce with chunky sourdough.

4 lamb shanks
sea salt
flour, for dusting
3 tablespoons olive oil
4 garlic cloves, crushed
1 onion, diced
1 leek, thinly sliced
1 carrot, diced
2 celery stalks, diced
1 red chilli, deseeded and
    finely chopped
2 teaspoons smoked paprika
sea salt and freshly ground
    black pepper
2 tablespoons tomato paste
250 ml (1 cup) red wine
2 x 400 g cans whole or
    diced tomatoes
1 litre (4 cups) beef stock
1 bouquet garni (see note)
sourdough, to serve
thyme and parsley leaves,
    to serve

Sweet potato mash

2 sweet potatoes (about 500 g),
    peeled and cut into 2 cm cubes
½ pumpkin, peeled, deseeded
    and cut into 2 cm cubes
    (chopped weight 500 g)
1 tablespoon ghee
pinch of nutmeg
sea salt and freshly ground
    black pepper

Season the lamb shanks with sea salt and dust with flour.

Heat 2 tablespoons of olive oil in a large, heavy-based saucepan over medium heat and fry the lamb shanks two at a time until golden brown on all sides. Remove from the pan and set aside.

Add the remaining olive oil to the pan and fry the garlic, onion, leek, carrot, celery, chilli, smoked paprika and a couple of pinches of salt and pepper, stirring frequently, until the vegetables have softened. Next, add the tomato paste and cook for another minute. Pour in the wine and bring to the boil, cooking for a few minutes to reduce slightly – it will smell divine. Add the tomatoes, stock, bouquet garni and lamb shanks. Bring to the boil, reduce the heat to low, cover and simmer for 4–5 hours. You just want the top of the sauce to be gently bubbling. By the time it's ready, the sauce will have reduced and thickened and the meat will be gorgeous, tender and falling off the bone.

To make the mash, cook the sweet potato and pumpkin in a saucepan of boiling water over medium heat for about 10 minutes or until soft. Turn off the heat, drain the vegetables in a colander and then return to the pan for another 30 seconds, to cook away any remaining moisture. Add the ghee and nutmeg and puree with a stick blender until you have a smooth and velvety consistency. If you're feeding a baby, set aside some of the puree (see note) then season the rest with salt and pepper.

Serve the mash in shallow bowls, topped with a lamb shank, a generous ladle of sauce and a slice of fresh sourdough on the side. Garnish with fresh thyme and parsley.

NOTES

• A bouquet garni is a lovely little bunch of herbs tied with kitchen string. I use 2 bay leaves, 2 thyme sprigs, 1 rosemary sprig and 3 flat-leaf parsley sprigs.

• If your baby has been on solids for a little while, you can add a tablespoon of lamb to the reserved mash and puree again.

BUCKWHEAT AND HERB FETTUCCINE WITH CARAMELISED ONION, BRUSSELS SPROUTS AND RAINBOW CHARD

SERVES 4–6

I love pasta and a lot of the time I'll happily cook it out of a packet. But, if I have time to make my own then I do, because it's one of those things that takes the dish to another level – the effort is well worth the return! Despite its name, buckwheat is actually a seed and deliciously nutty in taste. The addition of parsley is not only tasty but gives the fettuccine a lovely colour. I enjoy this with a funky orange wine.

1 tablespoon olive oil
1 bunch of rainbow chard, stalks
    sliced, leaves thickly shredded
400 g brussels sprouts,
    thinly sliced
zest and juice of 1 lemon

Buckwheat fettucine

300 g (2 cups) buckwheat flour
100 g (⅔ cup) tipo 00 flour
    (see note)
1 teaspoon salt
1 teaspoon freshly ground
    black pepper
1 tablespoon chopped flat-leaf
    parsley leaves
4 eggs
semolina, for rolling and
    sprinkling

Caramelised onion

25 g salted butter
1 tablespoon olive oil
2 large onions, halved and sliced
2 garlic cloves, crushed
2 tablespoons sherry or balsamic
    vinegar
1 tablespoon rapadura sugar

To serve

toasted walnuts, roughly
    chopped
flat-leaf parsley leaves
extra-virgin olive oil
shaved parmesan

To make the buckwheat fettuccine, place the flours, salt, pepper and parsley in a food processor and process for 15 seconds. Add the eggs and process for another 30 seconds, or until the dough comes together. Remove the dough from the processor, shape into a flat disc, wrap in plastic wrap, and refrigerate for 30 minutes to rest.

Divide the dough into quarters and, using a pasta machine or rolling pin, roll out as thinly as possible into long sheets, sprinkling with semolina to prevent the pasta sticking. Using a pasta machine or sharp knife, cut the dough into strips to make fettuccine. Sprinkle with more semolina, cover with plastic wrap and refrigerate until required.

To make the caramelised onion, heat the butter and oil in a large frying pan over medium heat. Add the onion and garlic and cook, stirring occasionally, for 15 minutes or until soft and golden. Add the vinegar and sugar, and cook for a further 5–6 minutes until caramelised. Transfer to a bowl and set aside until needed.

To cook the pasta, bring a large saucepan of salted water to a rolling boil. Add the pasta and cook, stirring, for 2–3 minutes or until al dente. Drain.

Heat the oil in a frying pan over high heat. Add the chard and brussels sprouts and stir-fry for 1–2 minutes or until the chard is just wilted. Return the onions to the pan and add the pasta, lemon zest and juice and stir gently until combined. Divide among serving bowls and top with the walnuts, parsley and a good drizzle of olive oil. Season with salt and pepper and finish with a sprinkle of shaved parmesan.

NOTE

The Italian tipo 00 flour ('farina tipo 00') is a finely milled plain flour suitable for pasta. You can get it from large supermarkets. If not, use strong flour or bread flour.

THE MULLUM CURRY

SERVES 4

The farmers' markets in the Byron Bay region are excellent thanks to passionate farmers who grow some of the most delicious produce I've ever tasted. One of my favourite markets is in Mullumbimby. It's a social gathering as much as a weekly shop, with everyone chatting away and tucking into coffee and market food under a big, beautiful fig tree. And not a mobile phone in sight! Vegetarian cuisine is big up in this neck of the woods, and this curry is a celebration of the amazing market vegetables that inspire me so much. It takes less than 30 minutes to make but packs a punch in terms of flavour and nutrition. I love it with brown rice and minty yoghurt. Thank you to all the farmers that nurture and grow our food!

200 g (1 cup) dried chickpeas
   (see note)
2 tablespoons yoghurt,
   whey or lemon juice
2 tablespoons coconut oil
12 curry leaves
2 teaspoons yellow
   mustard seeds
1 teaspoon cumin seeds
1 large onion, sliced
3 cm piece of ginger, finely grated
2 garlic cloves, crushed
1½ teaspoons ground coriander
1 teaspoon garam masala
½ teaspoon ground turmeric
pinch of ground cinnamon
2 long green chillies, sliced
2 tomatoes, finely chopped
50 g (½ bunch) coriander, roots
   and stems finely chopped,
   leaves reserved to serve
1 x 400 ml can coconut cream
400 g butternut pumpkin,
   peeled, deseeded and cut
   into 2 cm pieces
500 g cauliflower florets
200 g green beans, trimmed
   and halved
120 g baby spinach leaves
cooked brown rice, to serve
Minty cucumber yoghurt,
   to serve (see page 192)

Place the chickpeas in a bowl with plenty of water and 2 teaspoons of yoghurt, whey or lemon juice. Cover with a tea towel and leave to soak overnight. They will double in size, so you'll end up with about 2 cups of chickpeas.

The next day, drain and rinse the chickpeas and place in a saucepan. Add enough water to cover the chickpeas by about 3 cm. Bring to the boil, reduce the heat and cook, uncovered, for 1–1½ hours or until tender.

Heat the oil in a heavy-based saucepan over medium heat. Add the curry leaves and cook for 30 seconds until bright green and crisp. Use a slotted spoon to transfer the curry leaves to a plate. Set aside.

Add the mustard and cumin seeds to the pan and cook, stirring, for 1 minute until the seeds pop and become fragrant. Add the onion, ginger, garlic, coriander, garam marsala, turmeric, cinnamon and chilli and cook, stirring, for 3–4 minutes until the onion softens. Add the tomato, coriander roots and stems, coconut cream, pumpkin and cauliflower, and cook for a further 3–4 minutes until the vegetables soften. Stir in the beans, chickpeas and spinach, season and cook for a further 2 minutes or until the spinach has wilted and the vegetables are tender.

Spoon into serving bowls, top with the coriander and curry leaves and serve with brown rice. A dollop of minty cucumber yoghurt is a delicious offset to the heat and spice.

NOTE

If you can get your hands on a 2 cm piece of kombu or wakame (types of seaweed that you can find in most health-food stores), pop it into the liquid when you're soaking and cooking the chickpeas – it helps to soften them.

PEARL BARLEY RISOTTO WITH MUSHROOMS AND PECORINO

SERVES 4

I remember my mum and grandma using pearl barley to make hearty soups, and it's still one of my favourite grains. Its nuttiness and slightly chewy texture make it a perfect alternative to rice in risotto, and it goes beautifully with mushrooms and cheese. When I was young, the whole family would go mushroom picking every autumn, and we'd collect so many that my mum was always coming up with new and interesting ways to prepare them. I still find the aroma of cooking mushrooms absolutely divine. Any mushroom will shine in this risotto, but if you happen to have pine mushrooms they are an absolute treat. The best way to get pine mushrooms is to pick them yourself or you might find them at a farmers' market in autumn.

3 tablespoons olive oil

3 garlic cloves, crushed

1 onion, diced

1 leek, finely sliced

½ teaspoon ground nutmeg

300 g (1½ cups) pearl barley

250 ml (1 cup) white wine

1 litre (4 cups) chicken or
vegetable stock

1 bay leaf

10 sage leaves, chopped,
plus extra to serve

1 tablespoon chopped
thyme leaves

400 g mixed mushrooms,
chopped

zest of 1 lemon

100 g pecorino, shaved, plus
extra to serve

2 tablespoons crème fraîche
(see note; optional)

1 long red chilli, deseeded
and sliced

Heat 2 tablespoons of oil in a large saucepan over medium heat. Add two-thirds of the garlic, the onion, leek and nutmeg, and sauté until the onion is soft and translucent. Add the pearl barley and stir well to coat. Pour in the wine and simmer, stirring occasionally, for a couple of minutes until reduced slightly. Add the stock and bay leaf, partially cover and cook on a low simmer for about 40 minutes, until the liquid is almost absorbed.

About 10 minutes before the pearl barley risotto is ready, place the remaining 1 tablespoon of oil in another saucepan over medium heat. Add the remaining garlic, the sage and thyme and sauté for 1–2 minutes. Add the mushrooms and cook until brown, soft and fragrant.

When the risotto is ready, stir in the mushroom mixture, lemon zest and shaved pecorino. Remove from the heat and stir in the crème fraîche, if using. Garnish with extra pecorino, the sliced chilli and fresh sage leaves.

NOTE

Crème fraîche is basically a thicker, richer and less tangy version of sour cream. It's great in sauces as it can be heated without curdling. To make your own cultured cream at home, place 1 cup of pure cream (also known as pouring cream) in a clean jar. Stir in 1 tablespoon of buttermilk or yoghurt and cover with muslin. Leave it to culture and thicken for about 24 hours, ideally at around 25–30°C. It's ready once it's thick, at which point you can pop on a lid and keep it in the fridge for up to 2 weeks.

RUSTIC BEEF AND BARLEY STEW

SERVES 6

I came up with this recipe during the winter when I was pregnant, as I needed nourishing foods high in iron. You simply chop everything roughly and throw it all in the slow cooker and cook overnight or in the morning, and you have hearty, comforting dinners for days. Because the meat cooks so slowly, you don't need an expensive cut – in fact, the cheaper the better. But the quality of the beef is important, as you're drawing out every bit of goodness, so make sure it's pasture-raised and organic. Good-quality, organic bone broth or stock will make the dish more nourishing and tasty, but if you don't have any, water works quite well due to the slow cook. The addition of pearl barley creates a nice, rich texture, and because it's cooked for so long you don't need to pre-soak it. I like to freeze a couple of portions, as it makes a great pie filling, too.

1 kg beef (e.g. chuck or gravy
    beef), cubed
1 white onion, roughly chopped
3 garlic cloves, crushed
2 carrots, roughly chopped
500 g mushrooms, sliced
1 x 400 g can whole tomatoes
1 rosemary sprig
2 flat-leaf parsley sprigs,
    plus extra leaves to serve
500 ml (2 cups) beef stock
    or water
sea salt and freshly ground
    black pepper
100 g (½ cup) pearl barley

Preheat the slow cooker while you chop and prepare your ingredients.

Place all of the ingredients except the barley in the slow cooker. If the beef and vegetables aren't fully covered, add some more water. Cover and cook on low for at least 8 hours. I have cooked it for almost 16 hours before, and the sauce and flavour were deliciously rich! Add the pearl barley in the last 2 or so hours of cooking. When the stew is ready, remove the rosemary and parsley sprigs with tongs. Serve the stew topped with fresh parsley leaves.

NOTE

To make beef and barley pies, divide the warm stew between ramekins or small ovenproof baking dishes and top with puff pastry. Brush the pastry with melted butter and sprinkle over some sesame seeds. Score the top of the pastry and bake at 180°C for 10–15 minutes, or until the pastry is crisp and golden brown.

DIY BEAUTY:
FEEDING YOUR SKIN NATURALLY

A few years ago I was working crazy hours in television, wearing lots of make-up and not getting much sleep, and I noticed rashes and irritation on my face. One day Darren said, 'Just stop putting crap on your skin.' It seems obvious now, but at the time it hadn't really occurred to me that some of the chemicals in the products I was using could have been responsible. Considering I still had to 'put my face on' for my job, I decided to give my beauty cabinet at home an overhaul and started making some of my own creams. My skin literally improved in a day and I've been using mostly natural skin products ever since. My skin has never felt healthier.

DRINK WATER

This isn't very exciting, but I have to say that drinking plenty of water makes a bigger difference to my skin than any cream or treatment by a mile. If you think about it, dried fruit like sultanas or goji berries become plump and supple once you soak them in water. It's the same with our skin!

EAT GOOD FATS

You are what you eat, so a diet with plenty of good fats from avocado, olive oil, nuts, oily fish and egg yolks does wonders for your skin. Collagen-rich bone broth (see my Healing Chicken Broth recipe on page 212) is also particularly good for healthy skin, hair and nails. For an extra dose of omega 3, I drizzle linseed oil on my porridge, too.

MAKE YOUR OWN BEAUTY PRODUCTS

It's so easy to make your face treatments at home using basic ingredients in the fridge or pantry. They're all natural, cheap and smell divine!

Coconut oil

One of my favourite all-purpose beauty products is coconut oil. Because it's solid at room temperature, it works great as a lip balm (and it doesn't matter if you eat it!). I also use it to remove make-up, as an under eye moisturiser and as a hydrating hair mask. In the summer, I massage it through my hair in the morning and tie it up in a bun so it can soak in all day (and remind me of holidays!). Then I wash it off when I shampoo in the evening.

Pore-refining lemon facial

Egg whites and lemon juice help to tighten pores. This combination is great for oily skin.

1 egg white
½ teaspoon honey
1 teaspoon lemon juice

Mix the ingredients in a small bowl and apply to the face and neck. Leave on for 10 minutes, then rinse off with lukewarm water and pat skin dry.

Moisturising oatmeal mask

You'll often see oatmeal in products for sensitive and allergy-prone skin due to its anti-inflammatory and moisturising properties. Vitamins A and E in olive oil are anti-ageing, the lactic acid in yoghurt helps to dissolve dead skin cells and the honey is anti-bacterial. Together, these ingredients can only mean luscious, glowing skin.

1 tablespoon oatmeal
1 teaspoon olive oil
1 tablespoon natural yoghurt
1 tablespoon honey

Combine all of the ingredients in a small bowl, smooth onto your skin and leave on for 10 minutes. Rinse well and pat dry.

Detoxing clay mask

Bentonite clay is formed from volcanic ash. When it's mixed with a liquid, it has a strong negative charge, which attracts any impurities that are positively charged and thus absorbs and removes them. The one to get is the food-grade bentonite so it doesn't matter if you accidentally swallow it – it's also used internally to cleanse the body and gut of heavy metals and toxins. Other benefits include healing skin tissue, unclogging pores and blackheads and preventing breakouts

1 tablespoon bentonite clay
2 tablespoons water

Place the water in a very small jar. Add the clay and leave it to sit for around 15 minutes to form a slurry. Pour off any excess water and then apply the mixture to your face. Leave for about 10 minutes – it will dry and become quite tight – then rinse off and pat dry.

Good morning coffee scrub

This is my favourite skin treatment for 'waking up' my skin when it's tired and dull. The coffee and cinnamon are stimulants, so they help to get the blood circulating, plus the granules provide a gentle exfoliating action. The coconut oil is super-hydrating and the honey is anti-bacterial. My skin feels fresher, softer and more radiant. I just have to stop myself from eating it because it smells so good!

1 tablespoon ground coffee
½ teaspoon ground cinnamon
½ tablespoon coconut oil
½ tablespoon honey

Mix all the ingredients together in a small bowl until well combined. Using your fingertips, gently massage into the skin in a circular motion for about a minute. Leave for 5–15 minutes and then rinse off thoroughly with lukewarm water and pat dry.

Soothing fresh aloe vera gel

The best version of aloe vera gel is the one that comes straight from the plant. Fortunately, it's a hardy member of the cacti family, so it's quite easy to grow. Aloe vera is incredibly healing for sunburn and dry skin. Just snip one of the outer 'leaves' off your plant, slice of the spiky edges, peel the skin away and the gel will be revealed. Scoop it out and apply directly to sunburn or dry skin. There's no need to rinse it off. Store any leftover gel in a glass jar in the fridge.

ONE-POT WILD RICE AND CHICKEN PILAF

SERVES 4

We have a curry tree in our backyard, and I can't get enough of the aromatic leaves. So much so that I must cook with them every week. Inspired by their unique taste and smell, which funnily enough is nothing like curry, I came up with this Indian version of a wild rice and chicken pilaf. It's fragrant, hearty and spicy, yet you'll only need one pot and 15 minutes to prepare it. That's my kind of cooking! It's particularly delicious with a dollop of minty cucumber yoghurt, a few sprigs of coriander and some freshly squeezed lime juice.

50 g (¼ cup) coconut oil

⅓ cup small, fresh curry leaves

1 tablespoon ground turmeric

2 tablespoons ground coriander

2 tablespoons ground cumin

1 tablespoon brown mustard
seeds

1 large onion, halved and
thinly sliced

360 g (2 cups) wild rice,
well rinsed

1 litre (4 cups) chicken stock

1 x 1.8 kg whole chicken, skin
on, cut into 4 pieces (see note)

1 garlic bulb, halved crossways

juice of 1 lemon

Minty cucumber yoghurt

280 g (1 cup) Greek yoghurt

1 teaspoon sea salt

⅓ cup finely shredded mint leaves

1 Lebanese cucumber, deseeded
and finely chopped

1 tablespoon lime juice

1 long green chilli, deseeded
and finely chopped

To serve

lime wedges

coriander sprigs

Preheat the oven to 180°C.

Place a large heavy-based, flame-proof baking dish over medium heat. Add the oil. Once melted, add the curry leaves, spices and onion. Cook, stirring occasionally, for 5 minutes or until the onion is soft and light golden. Stir through the rice and stock and remove from the heat. Add the chicken, skin side up, then the garlic and lemon juice. Cover the dish tightly with two sheets of aluminium foil. Bake for 2 hours or until the rice and chicken are tender.

Meanwhile, make the minty cucumber yoghurt. Combine all of the ingredients in a small bowl and mix well. Set aside.

Remove the dish from the oven and increase the oven temperature to 220°C. Remove the foil and return the dish to the oven to bake for 10 minutes or until the chicken skin becomes crisp. Rest for 5 minutes, then serve with the minty cucumber yoghurt, lime wedges and coriander sprigs.

NOTES

- Ask your butcher to cut the chicken into two Maryland pieces (drumstick and thigh) and two breast on the bone with wing attached pieces.

- If you don't own a heavy-based, flame-proof baking dish, simply fry the oil, curry leaves, spices and onion in a separate small frying pan first and add to your baking dish along with the remaining ingredients.

SERVES 2

I've borrowed this ah-mazing risotto from one of my favourite cafes in Byron – Punch and Daisy in Mullumbimby, run by husband and wife Adam and Lara. They are champions of local produce and do it great justice with their exceptional coffee and tasty, hearty food – seriously, I could live on it! This risotto is a great alternative to conventional risotto, and Adam says it needs a strong arm! It requires preparing and cooking separate elements, but when combined it puts risotto back on the menu for everyone. Be sure to light some candles and crack open a delicious vino for this one.

200 g (1 cup) brown rice
   (see note)
500 ml (2 cups) vegetable stock
100 g (½ cup) tri-colour quinoa
good splash of extra-virgin olive
   oil, plus extra to serve
10 chestnut mushrooms, sliced
½ small onion, finely chopped
4 garlic cloves, crushed
1 celery stalk, finely chopped
6 thyme sprigs, leaves picked
splash of dry white wine
2 tablespoons cream
1 tablespoon butter
30 g parmesan, grated, plus
   extra to serve
dash of truffle oil, plus extra
   to serve
juice of ½ lemon
handful of parsley, chopped
sea salt and freshly ground
   black pepper

Enoki mushroom salad
50 g fresh enoki mushrooms
50 g (½ cup) shaved almonds,
   toasted
50 g snow pea tendrils (see note)
20 g marjoram leaves
30 g chopped flat-leaf parsley
   leaves
extra-virgin olive oil, for drizzling
squeeze of lemon juice

Place the brown rice in a small saucepan with 200 ml of the vegetable stock. Bring to the boil, then reduce the heat and simmer, covered, for 15–20 minutes, or until the stock has been absorbed.

In a separate small saucepan, cook the quinoa with 150 ml of the vegetable stock over medium heat, covered, for about 10 minutes, until it has fluffed up and sprouted little tails. Set aside.

Heat the olive oil in a heavy-based saucepan over high heat. Add the chestnut mushrooms and cook for about 5 minutes until browned. Turn the heat down to medium and add the onion, garlic, celery and thyme, and cook for 5 minutes or until the onion is translucent but not browned. Stir in the cooked rice and quinoa and the wine, and cook until the wine has been absorbed. Add a ladle (about ¼ cup) of the remaining vegetable stock and the cream, then simmer and stir for 5 minutes until absorbed. If needed, add more stock to achieve a loose, wet and creamy consistency. Remove from the heat and stir in the butter, parmesan, truffle oil, lemon juice and parsley. Season to taste.

In a separate bowl, combine the enoki mushrooms, almonds, pea tendrils, marjoram, parsley, olive oil and lemon juice, and season to taste. Spoon the risotto into shallow bowls and top with the enoki salad, followed by more grated parmesan, olive oil ... and an extra dash of truffle oil!

NOTES

• I use local, rain-fed biodynamic brown rice, which is grown locally in Nimbin. If you aren't able to source it, the next best option is organic brown rice.

• Snow pea tendrils (sometimes called pea tendrils or pea shoots) are the tips of young pea plants and are available from farmers' markets, grocers and some supermarkets.

ZUCCHETTI AND MEATBALLS

SERVES 4

This is the dish I make when I feel like spaghetti and meatballs but want something a little lighter. Zucchini make the perfect noodles and the meatballs are a reinvention of my mum's amazing rissoles, so you can use the recipe to make burgers, too. All that's left to make is a delicious, simple red sauce and while that's simmering, pop on your comfiest clothes and favourite film and then tuck in. If I'm having a glass of red, I like to add a splash to the sauce for extra flavour, but only if I'm cooking for adults!

5–6 large zucchini

oil, for frying

grated parmesan, to serve

½ cup basil leaves, to serve

Meatballs

500 g pork or beef mince

1 white onion, finely diced

1 egg, lightly beaten

3 tablespoons breadcrumbs
   soaked in 185 ml (¾ cup) water

2 tablespoons finely chopped
   flat-leaf parsley leaves

1 tablespoon thinly sliced
   spring onion

1 tablespoon chopped dill fronds

sea salt and freshly ground
   black pepper

Simple red sauce

2 tablespoons grapeseed oil

1 white onion, diced

2 garlic cloves, crushed

500 g (2 cups) passata

2 tablespoons tomato paste

3 tomatoes, roughly chopped

90 g mushrooms, sliced

Place the meatball ingredients in a bowl and mix by hand until well combined. Roll heaped tablespoonfuls of the mixture into about 14 balls, pop on a plate and set aside.

To make the sauce, heat the oil in a saucepan over medium heat. Add the onion and garlic and cook for a few minutes until soft and fragrant. Add the passata, tomato paste, tomato and mushrooms, and cook for another few minutes until the mushrooms are soft. Now gently place the meatballs in the sauce (they should be almost covered), reduce the heat and gently simmer for about 30 minutes. Give the mixture a gentle stir every 5–10 minutes to ensure that the meatballs cook evenly.

Meanwhile, use a spiraliser to make your zucchini noodles. Just before serving, heat a little oil in a frying pan over medium–high heat and flash-fry the noodles for 1–2 minutes until warm. Serve immediately in shallow bowls, topped with meatballs, sauce, parmesan and fresh basil leaves.

Any leftover meatballs and sauce will keep in an airtight container in the fridge for up to 2 days.

BUCKWHEAT AND WINTER FRUIT CRUMBLE

SERVES 6

Fruit crumble is the ultimate comforting winter dessert and such a perfect way to showcase the season's best fruits. I can never choose between apples, pears and rhubarb, so I use all three and love the addition of buckwheat, nuts and LSA in the crumble. It must be served deliciously warm, and it would be rude not to have it with vanilla ice cream or thick cream.

40 g butter

3 green apples, peeled, cored and thickly sliced

2 firm pears, peeled, cored and thickly sliced

500 g rhubarb, cut into 5 cm pieces

2 tablespoons honey

1½ teaspoons ground ginger

½ teaspoon ground cinnamon

Crumble topping

75 g (½ cup) buckwheat flour

55 g (⅓ cup) coconut sugar

2 tablespoons LSA (see note)

120 g cold butter, diced

85 g (½ cup) cooked, chilled buckwheat

30 g (⅓ cup) rolled oats

35 g (¼ cup) slivered almonds

vanilla ice cream or thick cream, to serve

Melt the butter in a large heavy-based frying pan over medium–high heat. Add the apple and pear and cook, stirring frequently, for 2–3 minutes. Add the rhubarb and cook for a further 2 minutes, or until the fruit starts to soften but still retains its shape. Stir in the honey, ginger and cinnamon, and cook for 2 minutes or until caramelised. Transfer the fruit and any pan juices to a 2 litre-capacity (8 cup) ovenproof dish. Set aside for 10 minutes to cool.

Preheat the oven to 200°C.

While the fruit is cooling, make the crumble topping by placing the flour, sugar, LSA and butter in a large bowl. Using your fingertips, rub the butter into the dry ingredients until the mixture resembles breadcrumbs. Add the cooked buckwheat, oats and almonds, and continue rubbing until the mixture forms small clumps. Scatter the crumble over the fruit and bake for 30 minutes or until golden. Serve with cream or ice cream.

NOTE

LSA is a mixture of linseeds (also called flaxseeds), sunflower seeds and almonds. It can be found in most supermarkets.

OLD FASHIONED VANILLA MARSHMALLOWS

MAKES 25

Since moving to Byron, one of our favourite things to do is catch up with friends on the beach and toast marshmallows over a campfire. Marshmallows are such simple treats, yet so satisfying – especially when you've made them yourself! Now, I'll be the first to admit that they're not the most nutritious treat, but I've tried using unrefined sweeteners like honey and rapadura sugar and they just didn't taste right. My philosophy is that it's a bit of a rare treat, so I may as well indulge in the real thing! It only takes about 15 minutes to whip them up, but it's important to be very organised and precise (you'll need a sugar thermometer and a stand mixer). I recommend having all of your ingredients measured out, your equipment ready to go and to mentally rehearse the steps before you do them. But don't let this put you off. Once you've made them the first time, you'll fall in love with the perfect, pillowy texture and sweet, melt-in-your mouth fluffiness.

6¼ gelatine leaves

2 egg whites

260 g caster sugar, divided into 185 g and 75 g portions

1 vanilla pod, split and seeds scraped (or 2 teaspoons vanilla paste)

40 g (¼ cup) icing sugar, sifted, for dusting

35 g (¼ cup) cornflour, sifted, for dusting

Place the gelatine leaves in a bowl of cold water to soak for 5 minutes.

Meanwhile, line a 20 cm x 20 cm baking tray with baking paper. Place the egg whites in the bowl of your stand mixer with a whisk attachment and move the mixer close to the stove. Also place the 75 g portion of caster sugar in a small bowl near the mixer.

To make your sugar syrup, place the 185 g portion of caster sugar in a saucepan with 100 ml of water over medium heat until it reaches 127°C. This usually takes about 5 minutes so while you're waiting, squeeze out any excess water from your softened gelatine leaves and place them in a bowl over the saucepan to melt. When the sugar syrup reaches 118°C on your sugar thermometer, start whisking the egg whites on high speed until they forms soft peaks. With the mixer still whisking, slowly pour in the 75 g of caster sugar. The mixture will start to look like meringue. When the sugar thermometer reaches 127°C, take the sugar syrup off the heat and stir in the melted gelatine and vanilla. With the mixer whisking, slowly pour in the gelatine and sugar syrup mixture down the inside of the bowl. When it's all in, keep whisking for another 7 minutes or so until the mixture has cooled down. It will be like a meringue but oozy and sticky.

Using a spatula, transfer the mixture to the prepared tray and smooth it out. Don't worry if it's not perfect – they are homemade after all! Place the tray in the fridge for at least 2 hours to set.

In a bowl, mix together the sifted icing sugar and cornflour.

Slowly peel the baking paper away from the edges of the tray and cut the marshmallow into 4 cm squares. It will be wobbly and sticky. If the knife sticks, dip it in the icing sugar mixture. Dip each marshmallow in the icing sugar mixture and place on a plate.

Now make a hot chocolate, dunk a marshmallow on top and enjoy in your comfiest chair! The marshmallows will keep in a sealed container for up to 2 weeks.

COMPOSTING

Let's talk about soil for a minute. Sexy I know, but stay
with me! I never really gave soil much thought until
I started my own veggie patch. I used to think
it was just, well, dirt; a sort of sponge that holds things
together. But I've since come to appreciate that it's so
much more than that, it's a living, breathing community!

One of my favourite books on the subject is *The Third Plate* by chef Dan Barber
(by the way, if you're interested in the future of food and farming, this is a must-
read). He says that one teaspoon of soil has over a million, even a billion, living
organisms! When I think about it this way, the link between the quality of the soil
and the health of the plants becomes very obvious. And the necessity to feed this
soil plenty of organic matter from compost and mulch is essential. Organic matter
not only provides nutrients for plants, but also improves the structure of the soil
making it more friable with more air spaces, which allows water to penetrate more
deeply and more quickly.

Making your own compost is such a satisfying way to transform your green
waste into nourishment for your garden. And even if you don't have a garden, or it's
too small to cope with all of your compost, you can always give it to your community
garden. Better still, you can set up a small worm farm somewhere like your balcony.
Our worm farm is under the house, and they go through all of our green waste!
What's left behind is an extremely nutrient-rich liquid (or 'worm tea') that we use
to water our plants, and they are thriving! I'm not going to lie though, the worms
aren't really my cup of tea (so to speak), so this is Darren's job!

HOW TO MAKE YOUR OWN COMPOST

Composting can seem a bit overwhelming when you're starting out (it was for me),
so I've simplified it into 10 easy steps. The trick to successful composting is balance.
It's like baking a cake – you don't want too many wet ingredients or too many dry
ingredients. So if your compost is starting to get sludgy or smelly, just add some dry
material, like leaves, twigs or even shredded paper. If it's too dry, keep adding the
kitchen scraps with a little water.

Materials

› container for kitchen scraps (with a lid)
› compost bin (200-litre or 400-litre)
› chicken wire or rabbit-proof mesh
› dried leaves and twigs
› green garden clippings (leaves and grass, but not weeds)
› soil
› water
› compost aerator (or garden fork)
› mulch

STEP 1 The first thing you need is a container with a lid for all your scraps. The lid is important to ensure that the scraps don't attract insects or vermin.

STEP 2 Get the household together and explain the new do's and don'ts:

› DO add household vegetable and fruit scraps along with coffee grounds, garden clippings, leaves and twigs.

› DO put citrus skins in there, but only a couple here and there. If you're juicing, you're better off putting the peels out in the sun and drying them to use as fire starters.

› DO put onion skins in there, but not at the start, and not too many (you should be okay unless you're eating onion bhajis every night!).

› DON'T put the following in your bin: dairy products; meat or fish; bread, pasta or rice; bones; oils, greases and fats; nuts; weeds; faeces; sauces and dressings; barbecue ash or coal.

STEP 3 If you go with a standard 200 or 400-litre black bin, place it in the garden on top of a piece of rabbit-proof mesh or chicken wire. This prevents any vermin from digging into it from below (though if you keep the right balance of wet/dry, you shouldn't get any).

STEP 4 Gather some dried leaves and twigs and place them in a 15–20 cm layer at the bottom of the bin. Add about 5 litres of water (half a watering can), or 10 litres if you're using a bigger bin.

STEP 5 Next, add a shovelful of some green material, such as garden clippings from shrubs or trees, or even some grass clippings mixed with leaves and water that in. This is your 'base'.

STEP 6 Place a shovelful of garden soil on top – this contains all the bacteria that help break things down. Add a shovelful of compost, too, if available.

STEP 7 Now add another shovelful of dry material, such as dried leaves, grass or twigs, to balance the green food scraps that you'll be adding every couple of days. I call this the 'brown layer' or carbon layer. Some people add dried coffee grounds to the dry material, too, but these need to be added in equal proportions to the other brown ingredients.

STEP 8 Add your first bucket of scraps from the kitchen, water them in with your watering can and then add the equivalent amount of brown material, making sure the green is well covered. Water again, then throw a dusting of soil over the top, and that's the beginning of your composting process.

STEP 9 Keep adding your layers until the bin is full, making sure that you water in your scraps each time to keep the compost just damp (but not wet).

STEP 10 When the bin is full, turn it with an aerator (they look like a giant cork-screw) or garden fork once a week. Do this for about eight weeks and the compost will be ready to go. (It may take a couple of weeks longer in cold weather.)

Don't worry if your compost is not perfectly uniform – simply remove any bigger chunks and put them back in the bottom of the bin as starters for your next batch. It will encourage the growth of beneficial fungi and microbes and help fight off any pathogens – just like the constant balancing act that goes on in our gut flora!

Now it's time to spread the compost over your garden soil and dig it in. You then need to cover the compost with a layer of mulch, so the compost doesn't dry out and lose its fertility-building and moisture-holding capacity. It won't be long before your plants flourish!

RAINY

RECIPES FOR REJUVENATION,
PICKLING, BAKING, PRESERVING.

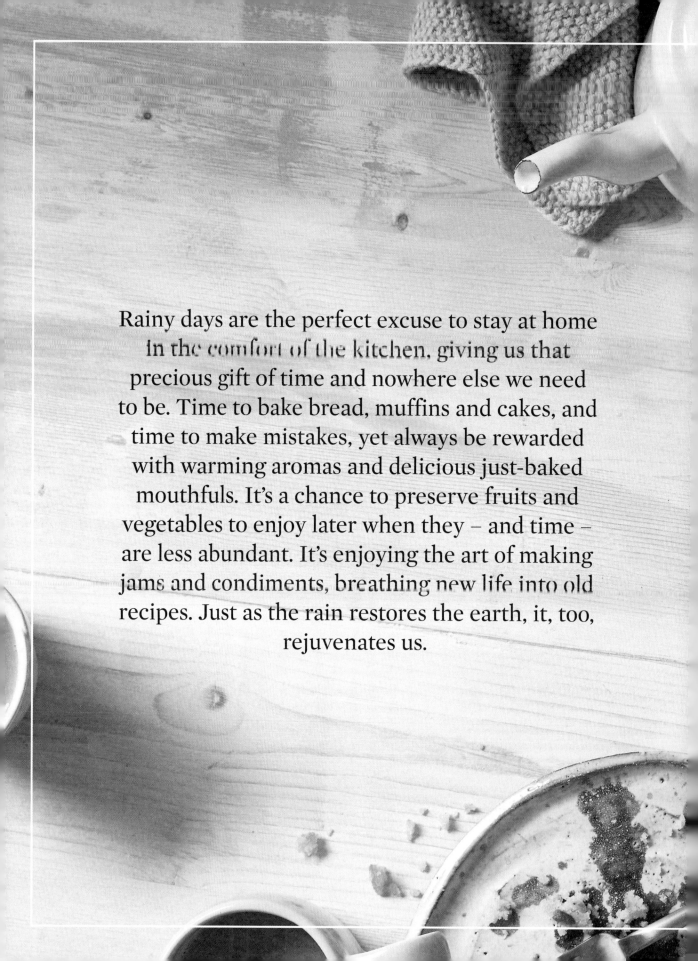

Rainy days are the perfect excuse to stay at home in the comfort of the kitchen, giving us that precious gift of time and nowhere else we need to be. Time to bake bread, muffins and cakes, and time to make mistakes, yet always be rewarded with warming aromas and delicious just-baked mouthfuls. It's a chance to preserve fruits and vegetables to enjoy later when they – and time – are less abundant. It's enjoying the art of making jams and condiments, breathing new life into old recipes. Just as the rain restores the earth, it, too, rejuvenates us.

Chicken broth is one of the most nutritious, healing foods on the planet. It's an immune booster, digestion aid and super-tonic for glowing skin, hair and nails. It's also particularly nourishing during pregnancy and afterwards for replenishing your body. Your bone broth should end up much thicker than your normal soup broth because you're cooking the bones for much longer (12–24 hours), allowing them to release their incredible nutrients. A good broth will solidify when it's in the fridge because it's so gelatinous, but it will go runny again once you heat it up. It's the perfect thing to make in the slow cooker overnight or when you're at work. Drink it as is, or reheat it and add fresh veggies like carrots, kale and broccoli. Daz does a great Asian version by adding spring onions, chilli, basil and coriander, along with a little soy sauce and lemon juice. I always freeze some, as it comes in handy for anything that calls for stock, such as stews, sauces and risotto. Adding a couple of tablespoons of stock to a baby's pureed veggies is a wonderful way of adding nutrients to their first foods. It also makes a great 'hidden' superfood in pasta sauces, soups and sauces for older children.

2 chicken feet (optional; see note)

1 kg chicken bones (see note)

1 onion, roughly chopped

2 carrots, scrubbed and roughly chopped

2 celery stalks, roughly chopped

1 bunch of flat-leaf parsley, roughly chopped

6 garlic cloves, roughly chopped

2 tablespoons apple cider vinegar

4 bay leaves

1 teaspoon black peppercorns

1 teaspoon sea salt

If you're using chicken feet, blanch them to 'sterilise' them and remove any impurities. Do this by placing them in a saucepan of cold water and bringing to the boil over high heat. Remove from the heat, drain and transfer to a large stockpot.

Place the chicken bones in the stockpot and pour in about 6 litres of water. The liquid needs to clear the bones by about 5 cm. Bring to the boil and skim off any impurities that have risen to the surface. Reduce the heat to the lowest setting possible (or transfer the bones and liquid to a slow cooker). Add the remaining ingredients, cover and cook for 12–24 hours. Skim off any impurities if you happen to notice them.

Allow to cool slightly then strain the liquid through a fine sieve to remove the bones and veggie bits. The stock will keep in the fridge for 5–7 days and up to 3 months in the freezer.

NOTES

• Chicken feet are amazing for this broth, because they're so rich in gelatine and collagen, but make sure that they're not bleached. That's right, chicken feet are sometimes bleached in peroxide to disinfect them and make them look whiter, but you definitely don't want to be putting that chemical in your body! Just ask your butcher when you buy them.

• You can buy chicken bones and carcasses from your butcher. They are cheap, too! It's important that the bones are from humanely raised chooks fed on organic, chemical-free and hormone-free chook food, as you're extracting and ingesting minerals from them in a concentrated form. Just check with your butcher when you go to buy the bones. Veggies should be organic, too.

My inspiration for this recipe came from my friend, Grant, who happens to be a chef, horticulturist and wellness advocate. He grows all sorts of amazing vegetables and herbs on his property, and one day he dropped around some turmeric paste just as all of us came down with nasty colds. We drank it as 'golden mylk' (an ancient Ayurvedic healing drink; see recipe below) and it did the trick within two days! Everyone needs a batch of this incredible stuff in their fridge, not only for its health benefits, but also for its delicious flavour (it can be added to everything from stews and soups to curries and teas). It's really important to consume it properly to get the anti-inflammatory and antioxidant benefits from its active ingredient, curcumin. Curcumin molecules are fat-soluble, so turmeric needs to be eaten with good fats such as coconut or olive oil to get all the benefits. Adding black pepper also enhances the bioavailability of curcumin by as much as 2000 per cent. This recipe makes three jars: one for the fridge, one for the freezer and one for a friend.

3 tablespoons coconut oil

150 g fresh turmeric, sliced

75 g ginger, sliced

1 tablespoon freshly ground
   black pepper

juice of 1 lemon

1 tablespoon ground cinnamon

1 tablespoon ground fennel seeds

300 g honey

Melt 2 tablespoons of the coconut oil in a frying pan over medium heat. Add the turmeric, ginger and pepper and sauté for 3 minutes. Remove from the heat.

Transfer the warm turmeric mixture to a food processor with 125 ml (½ cup) water, the lemon juice and remaining tablespoon of coconut oil, and blitz to a puree. Add the cinnamon and ground fennel seeds and pulse to combine. Leave the mixture to cool.

Add the honey and mix until it forms a beautiful, golden paste. Spoon around 200 g of the paste into each jar and seal. Enjoy some immediately in Golden Mylk (see below). The paste keeps well in the fridge for at least 2 weeks.

GOLDEN MYLK

MAKES 1

1 cup almond milk (for a recipe
   see page 47)

1 tablespoon turmeric paste
   (see above)

honey, to serve (optional)

ground cinnamon, to serve

Place the almond milk and turmeric paste in a small saucepan over medium heat and stir for around 30 seconds or until it's warm. Alternatively, if you have a coffee machine, place the paste in a mug or cup, heat the milk in a jug using the steamer wand and pour the frothy milk over the paste, stirring gently to combine. Add some more honey if you like and sprinkle with cinnamon. You can pour your golden mylk through a sieve if you don't want any of the 'bits' floating around, but I recommend drinking them as that's how you'll get the most nutritional benefit. It's best enjoyed under a blanket with a good book.

RESTORATIVE PIG TROTTER AND PEANUT SOUP

SERVES 4-6

I first heard about the incredible restorative benefits of pig trotters from my acupuncturist, Marlene Farry, who was treating me for post-pregnancy depletion, by helping me replenish my body and boost my milk supply. In China, pig trotter soup is part of a new mother's 'confinement' diet, which is a 30-day long period of rest and recuperation where women look after new mums by cooking nourishing meals and helping with cleaning, among other things. According to traditional Chinese medicine, this soup warms the body and stimulates the production of breastmilk. Chinese women and Marlene swear by it – and it worked for me. It makes sense as pig trotters are very rich in collagen, minerals and vitamins. Inspired by the Chinese recipes, I created this version, which can be enjoyed as a broth or bulked up with vegetables and rice noodles as a meal on its own. Nutrients aside, it's very delicious.

140 g (1 cup) peanuts

1 pig trotter, cut into pieces (ask your butcher to do this)

1 tablespoon grapeseed oil

3 chicken carcasses, cut into pieces (ask your butcher to do this)

1 onion, peeled and quartered

1 garlic bulb, halved crossways

200 ml Shaoxing wine (Chinese cooking wine) (see note)

2 cm piece of ginger, finely chopped

1 teaspoon black peppercorns

1 long red chilli, thinly sliced

1 cup sliced mushrooms (any kind)

1 bunch of Chinese spinach, roughly chopped (see note)

200 g rice noodles

bean sprouts, to serve

handful of coriander leaves, to serve

Preheat the oven to 200°C.

Place the peanuts in a bowl, cover with water and leave to soak.

Meanwhile, blanch the pig trotter by placing it in a saucepan of cold water and bringing it to the boil. Remove from the heat, drain, transfer to a large stockpot and set aside. (This sterilises the trotter and removes any impurities.)

Place the oil, chicken carcasses, onion and garlic in a flame-proof ceramic dish or ovenproof saucepan and roast in the oven for 30 minutes or until golden brown. Transfer the carcasses, onion and garlic to the stockpot, drain the fat from the baking dish and deglaze with the Shaoxing wine (see note).

Add the glaze, ginger, peppercorns and chilli to the stockpot and cover with water. Bring to the boil, skimming off any impurities. Reduce the heat to low, cover and simmer for 6–12 hours. Strain the mixture through a fine sieve, discarding the solids, then return the broth to the stockpot.

Rinse and drain the soaked peanuts and add them to the broth. Just before serving, add the mushrooms, spinach and rice noodles and cook for a further 5 minutes. Serve topped with fresh bean sprouts and coriander leaves.

NOTES

- You can find Shaoxing wine and Chinese spinach at Asian grocers and most supermarkets.

- Deglazing is basically a way of making sure you get all the tasty bits from a frying pan or baking dish after you've cooked some meat, fish or vegetables in it. Remove the main cooked ingredient, place the baking dish or pan over high heat and add a liquid such as wine, stock or water. Scrape and stir it all around for a few minutes to get all the yummy fats and juices to melt and reduce. It ends up being a small amount of liquid but one that is full of flavour. It's usually used as a sauce or, in this case, transferred to a soup.

KALE, BASIL AND ROASTED HAZELNUT PESTO

MAKES ABOUT 2½ CUPS

A good pesto is one of those staples I always have knocking about in the fridge, as it ensures I can make a quick and delicious meal out of anything. Whether it's pasta, eggs or a humble toast with avocado, pesto makes everything taste better. It's also a great way to include nutrient-rich foods such as kale and garlic in your diet. The roasted hazelnuts in this recipe are such a treat, and I love them a little chunky to give the pesto a bit of crunch.

70 g (½ cup) hazelnuts

1 cup chopped kale, stems removed

125 ml (½ cup) olive oil

sea salt and freshly ground black pepper

80 g (1 cup firmly packed) basil leaves

50 g manchego or parmesan, grated

1 garlic clove, roughly chopped

juice of ½ lemon

Preheat the oven to 180°C.

Place the hazelnuts on a tray lined with baking paper and roast for about 15 minutes or until golden and fragrant.

Meanwhile, massage the chopped kale with a splash of the oil and a little sea salt for about 2 minutes until soft. (This removes the bitterness from the kale and makes it much tastier. You can use this technique when adding kale to your salads, too.)

When the hazelnuts are ready, remove them from the oven and place in a clean tea towel to steam for about a minute. Use the tea towel to rub the skins off the hazelnuts, as they can be a little bitter. (Don't worry if some skins don't come loose.) Place the hazelnuts in a food processor and blitz until coarse – you want them to be a little chunky, like crunchy peanut butter. Transfer to a bowl and set aside.

Place the kale, basil, cheese, garlic and half of the remaining olive oil in the food processor and blitz until it forms a puree. Add a teaspoon or so of the lemon juice, pulse to mix and taste it before adding any more as it can be overpowering. Add some more oil, too, if you prefer your pesto runnier. Season to taste with salt and pepper and stir through the roasted hazelnuts.

Spoon the pesto into a super-clean jar, packing the mixture down so there are no air bubbles. Cover with the remaining oil (this helps to preserve it).

Stir the pesto through your favourite pasta, spread on toasted sourdough or mix through scrambled eggs. Yum! The pesto will keep in the fridge for up to 2 weeks.

MAKE YOUR OWN TEA

Drinking herbal tea is a part of my daily ritual. I have a few cups each day, starting with fresh peppermint to wake me up and ending with soothing chamomile to relax and encourage a good night's sleep. What I have in between depends on how I'm feeling and what I need. A lot of the time, it's just a little comfort break and a moment to breathe. If it's energy I need, I'll have green tea, or for an immune boost it might be vitamin C–rich rosehip, echinacea or lemon and ginger.

My tea pantry is almost like a little medicine cabinet with all sorts of beautiful herbs and flowers, many of them I have grown myself.

MY FAVOURITE TEA FLAVOURS

Herbs: mint, rosemary, lemon balm
Flowers: chamomile, lavender, rosehip
Citrus: lemon, mandarin, orange, grapefruit, lemongrass
Spices: vanilla, cinnamon, cardamom, clove, fennel, star anise

GROW YOUR OWN HERBAL TEA GARDEN

There are many benefits to growing and making your own tea, not least of which is that you know that it's completely clean and natural. Homemade teas also make a beautiful gift. (See drying teas overleaf.)

You can grow your own tea herbs and flowers separately, but I find that they look beautiful clustered together in a garden bed, large pot or in small pots beside each other. If you do grow your herbs or flowers in pots, make sure you group together ones that like the same growing conditions. For example, I have my lavender and chamomile in a pot with some edible flowers, including dianthus and violas. They look gorgeous!

Mint: relaxation, digestion

Mint is particularly fast growing and can take over the garden bed, so this can be a good one to have in its own pot. Unlike other herbs, it likes a bit of shade and lots of water, especially in the summer when it will need it daily. Give it a good trim regularly or it goes wild!

Rosemary: memory, antioxidants, anti-inflammatory

Rosemary is drought tolerant and low maintenance. It enjoys cool, wet winters and warm to hot, dry summers, so it's best not to overwater.

Lemon balm: stress, colds, low mood

Lemon balm looks a lot like mint (it's from the same family) but has the most delicious, zesty lemon flavour. It likes to grow in cooler weather and spreads from its underground roots, so it's best to keep it in its own pot. It prefers well-drained soil, regular watering and lots of sunshine, so windowsills and patios are good spots.

Chamomile: stress, insomnia

Chamomile looks and tastes beautiful and is actually very low maintenance. It thrives in full sun or part shade and only needs watering around once a week. Camomile usually flowers in summer, so that's when you can enjoy the fresh flowers. They make a beautiful garnish on salads and muesli.

English lavender: insomnia, perfume, antiseptic

The scent of lavender is so delicate and fragrant, yet the plant itself is so hardy! A spot in full sun with good drainage and dry, warm weather is best as humidity and wet soil can bring on mould.

USING FRESH HERBS AND PLANTS TO MAKE TEA

If you're using fresh leaves or blossoms, you'll need a little more than you would use with dried leaves (around 2 teaspoons' worth). Place them in your cup, pour near-boiling water over them and steep for 3–5 minutes, bruising the leaves gently with a spoon to release the oils. You can sweeten with honey, if you wish.

Don't limit your blends to just one flavour. You can mix and match with a little zest from citrus fruits, such as lemon, mandarin, orange or grapefruit. Whole spices, such as vanilla, cinnamon sticks, cardamom pods, cloves, fennel seeds and star anise, all add delicious warmth and flavour. Simply add a pinch of fresh zest or spice to the cup.

DRYING YOUR OWN TEA

Drying your own tea is surprisingly simple and makes a gorgeous gift. Just bind the herbs or flowers in small bundles, ensuring that all the leaves and blossoms are exposed (not hidden underneath others), as this prevents them from becoming mouldy. It's best to tie the stems with a rubber band, as they will shrink as they dry and you don't want the middle ones falling out. I like to put a bit of kitchen string on top as it looks nicer. You can then hang them upside down on some kitchen string with pegs or tape them to a wall. They need to be in a spot where they can stay undisturbed from a few days to a few weeks. When the leaves become dry and crumbly, they are ready to store in an airtight jar. It's best not to crush them too much to preserve the oils. You can always crush them a little more just before steeping.

Alternatively, you can lay your leaves or blossoms on a paper towel, one-plant deep, in a cool, dry place and cover with muslin to protect them from dust and insects. Once they're dry, store in airtight jars where they will keep for 6–12 months.

PICKLED BLUEBERRIES

MAKES 1 X 500 ML JAR

I love blueberries! They're perfect in muesli and muffins, and I often like to snack on them with blue cheese, haloumi and nuts. This got me thinking that a pickled version would be ideal for adding that sweet tartness to salads and meats.

These look stunning on a cheese platter and also make a great accompaniment to roast pork. Pickling is also a great way to preserve berries to enjoy when they're not in season.

250 g blueberries
125 ml (½ cup) apple cider vinegar
55 g (¼ cup) demerara or raw sugar
1 tablespoon sea salt
5 whole cloves
1 cinnamon stick
1 star anise
1 teaspoon dried allspice berries

Wash the blueberries and set aside. Combine the remaining ingredients with 125 ml (½ cup) of water in a saucepan and bring to the boil. Turn down the heat and simmer for 10 minutes.

Meanwhile, sterilise the jar (see note).

Spoon the blueberries into the jar and cover with the pickling liquid, leaving at least 2 cm clear at the top. Seal the jar and store in the fridge for at least 3 days before eating.

NOTES

- To sterilise the jars, wash them in hot soapy water then rinse in hot water. Preheat the oven to 150°C. Boil the jars in a large stockpot of boiling water for 10 minutes. Drain them on a tea towel, then pop in the oven on a baking tray to dry. Remove the jars from the oven very carefully with tongs and an oven glove just before you're ready to use.

- If you want your blueberries softer and more like a chutney, simmer them with the vinegar and spices before transferring to the jar.

BEST EVER POLISH GHERKINS

MAKES 2 X 1 LITRE JARS

Now that's a big call I hear you say, but I was given this recipe from the master (my dad), so that settles that! He says it's all about the cucumber. He's been sourcing his from the same farmer – who grows them specifically for pickling alongside horseradish – for years. Dad says that if the cucumbers aren't organic and fresh, forget it – it won't matter what you add. Horseradish makes the cucumbers nice and crunchy, so if you can get some it's a bonus but not mandatory. Sourcing 'cherry leaves' is also slightly challenging, but bay leaves do the trick, too. Apart from that, it's just salt, peppercorns, garlic and dill. Making your own gherkins is incredibly simple and satisfying. Just don't skimp on the cucumbers! They are absolutely delicious eaten straight from the jar, on burgers or served as a side.

4 tablespoons salt
2 garlic cloves, chopped
4 dill fronds
2 x 2 cm pieces of horseradish (optional)
10 black peppercorns
2 bay leaves (or cherry leaves if you want to be a real Pole!)
1 kg small cucumbers

Place 2 litres (8 cups) of water and the salt in a saucepan over medium heat and bring to the boil. Remove from the heat and set aside for 10 minutes, or until warm.

Divide the garlic, dill, horseradish, peppercorns and bay leaves between 2 sterilised jars (see note at left) and then add the cucumbers, making sure they are packed in tightly, so that there's no chance they can float to the top and stick out of the brine. If this happens, they will spoil. Pour the warm salted water over the cucumbers, so that everything is well covered, leaving a 2-cm gap at the top of the jar.

Seal the jars tightly and leave them to pickle in a cool, dark place for at least a week, or longer if you can wait. Once open, they will keep in the fridge for a few weeks.

CARROT AND CARAWAY SAUERKRAUT

MAKES 2 X 750 ML JARS

I grew up eating sauerkraut. It was a side with virtually every savoury meal, alongside mustard of course! I had no idea of the health benefits of fermented foods as a kid – I just loved the zingy taste. But it was a way of life for my parents in Poland, especially during the freezing winters when most fresh foods weren't available. Preserving food by fermenting is much easier than you'd imagine (and cheap!) and a great way to use up extra fruits and vegetables to enjoy when they're not in season. Fermenting is different to pickling (where the acid (vinegar) preserves the food by inhibiting the growth of bacteria), because it actually encourages the growth of the good bacteria that convert the sugars and carbohydrates in the food to their own self-preserving acid (so in a sense it's pickled too!). Therefore, fermented foods not only offer that delicious tangy taste but also have great probiotic and nutritional value. Unfortunately, a lot of supermarket versions are pasteurised, which destroys a lot of these good bacteria (along with the taste), so I highly recommend making your own. It's a game changer! If you're going to commit to getting your fermentation on, it's worth investing in a good crock pot and some weights to create the optimal anaerobic environment for your fermentation. I love a little side of kraut in a breakfast bowl with eggs and leftover veggies, and it's delicious on a Reuben sandwich.

1 medium head of white cabbage (about 1 kg)

1 large carrot, grated

1½ tablespoons sea salt

4 bay leaves

5 black peppercorns

1 teaspoon caraway seeds, toasted

1 teaspoon coriander seeds, toasted

Pull the outer two leaves from the cabbage and reserve. Shred the rest of the cabbage using a sharp knife. Now place the cabbage, grated carrots and sea salt in a large bowl and massage with your hands for 10 minutes or so, until the vegetables start to soften and a brine starts to form.

Stuff the vegetables into 2 sterilised jars (see note on opposite page), pouring in the juice from the bottom of the bowl. Divide the bay leaves, peppercorns, caraway and coriander seeds evenly between the two jars. Press the vegetables down with your hands to remove any air pockets and submerge them under the juices. Fold up the reserved cabbage leaves and press them down on top of the vegetables to keep them under the brine. Secure the lids and pop the jars somewhere accessible, but out of direct sunlight. Wrap them in a tea towel if you like.

Loosen the lids on your jars every day for the first 5 days to release any carbon dioxide. Taste after the first week to see if the kraut is ready. (It takes longer if the weather is cooler.) It's ready when it has a slightly fizzy, tangy, beautifully sour taste. When you're happy with the taste, store the kraut in the fridge to inhibit any further fermentation. It should keep for about 6 months, but you'll probably finish it before then!

NOTE

If you're interested in fermentation, you might like to read *The Art of Fermentation* by Sandor Katz. He's the guru in this area, and I've found his book to be incredibly well researched and very inspiring.

Best-ever Polish gherkins

Pickled blueberries

Carrot and caraway sauerkraut

PUMPKIN BREAD

MAKES 1 LOAF

This pumpkin bread is Darren's favourite post-surf snack, so much so that he put it in his cookbook. I was chuffed! It's a great little loaf to bake on a rainy day and, unlike a lot of bread, is filling enough to use as a base for a meal. I particularly love it with avocado, feta and tomato. Or, for a sweeter version, ricotta and honey. The nuts and seeds are optional (you can replace them with any of your favourites), but I love them for the crunchy texture, fibre and good fats they add to the bread.

675 g (3 cups) grated pumpkin

3 eggs

1 tablespoon honey

2 tablespoons macadamia oil

generous pinch of salt

½ teaspoon ground nutmeg

½ teaspoon ground cinnamon

240 g (2 cups) almond meal

60 g (½ cup) coconut flour

1 tablespoon lemon juice

⅔ teaspoon bicarbonate of soda

80 g (⅔ cup) chopped pecans

4 tablespoons chia seeds

4 tablespoons sunflower seeds,
   plus extra for sprinkling

4 tablespoons pumpkin seeds,
   plus extra for sprinkling

Preheat the oven to 180°C. Grease a 25 cm loaf tin and line it with baking paper.

Place the pumpkin, eggs, honey and oil in a large bowl and mix well. Stir through the salt, nutmeg and cinnamon. Mix in the almond meal, coconut flour, lemon juice and bicarb soda. If the mixture feels too wet, add some more coconut flour. Gently fold through the pecans and seeds. Spoon into the prepared tin and sprinkle the top with the extra sunflower and pumpkin seeds. Bake for 1–1½ hours or until a skewer comes out clean.

Allow to cool in the tin before turning out onto a wire rack to cool completely.

NUT, SEED AND FIG BREAD

MAKES 1 LOAF

A good loaf of homemade, freshly baked bread is the holy grail, especially one made with spelt flour. To my mind, if you're going to go to the trouble of baking bread, you may as well go the whole hog and make a gorgeous one like this nut, seed and fig bread. It's perfect for a wholesome breakfast or afternoon tea and even more delicious with lashings of butter, ricotta and honey or my Strawberry and Chia Jam on page 247. If you happen to be entertaining, it's an impressive accompaniment to hard goat's cheese with honeycomb.

2 x 7 g sachets dried yeast

2 teaspoons honey

450 g (3 cups) wholemeal spelt flour (see note)

150 g (1 cup) bread flour, plus extra for dusting

1 tablespoon chia seeds

1 teaspoon sea salt

1½ teaspoons mixed spice

2 tablespoons macadamia oil

2 tablespoons semolina

250 g (1¼ cups) dried figs, roughly chopped

100 g (1 cup) walnuts, roughly chopped

2 fresh figs, thickly sliced

2 teaspoons milk

1 tablespoon rolled oats

1 tablespoon sunflower seeds

ricotta, to serve (for a recipe see page 86)

honey, to serve

Sprinkle the yeast over 375 ml (1½ cups) of lukewarm water, stir in the honey and set aside for 10 minutes or until frothy.

Place the flours, chia seeds, salt and mixed spice in a large bowl and stir well to combine. Pour in the yeast mixture and the oil. Using a palette knife or butter knife, stir until the mixture comes together. Turn out onto a clean, floured surface and knead for 3–4 minutes or until elastic and smooth. Return the dough to a large, lightly oiled bowl, cover with lightly oiled plastic wrap and a tea towel, and set aside in a draught-free place for 1–1½ hours to prove and double in size.

Preheat the oven to 210°C. Scatter the semolina on a baking tray.

Turn the dough out onto a lightly floured surface, knock back with your fist and scatter over the dried figs and walnuts. Knead the dough for 2 minutes until the figs and walnuts are well incorporated. Shape the dough into a loaf and place on the prepared tray. Make three diagonal slashes in the top of the loaf, and press fresh figs into the grooves. Set aside for 30 minutes to rise.

Brush the loaf with milk and sprinkle with oats and seeds. Bake for 25 minutes, then reduce the oven temperature to 190°C, and continue to bake for a further 20–25 minutes until golden and the bread sounds hollow when tapped underneath. Transfer to a wire rack to cool. Serve fresh or toasted with ricotta and honey or my jam on page 247.

NOTES

- The protein in spelt flour is more fragile than the protein in other flours, so it needs less kneading to become stretchy and elastic. If over-kneaded it can become spongy.
- You can substitute the dried figs with other dried fruit such as sour cherries.
- The bread will keep for 2–3 days in an airtight container, or can be wrapped in plastic and frozen for up to 2 months.

GRAINS, LEGUMES, NUTS AND SEEDS

Let's get technical for a moment. Grains, legumes, nuts and seeds are mini nutrient powerhouses, containing the protein and energy necessary to support new life. Nature has been very clever in creating systems that protect them from spoiling, and only allows them to germinate when the conditions are just right.

Unfortunately for us, these systems often include enzyme inhibitors that prevent us from digesting and breaking down the nutrients, as well as anti-nutrients, such as phytic acid, which bind to iron and other minerals and make them less bioavailable. Some of us are also sensitive to gluten (one of the proteins found in wheat, barley and rye), which can cause gut irritation. Yet, despite these protective systems, humans have been eating grains, legumes, nuts and seeds for millennia, and we've done it by working with nature to crack the code. Soaking the seeds sends them a message that conditions are ripe for germination, greatly increasing their digestibility. Fermenting them, even slightly, helps to break down the phytic acids and gluten even further. And it's not just about grains, ideally all legumes, seeds and nuts should be prepared properly, so that our bodies can access their precious nutrients.

However, food consumption has changed enormously over the last hundred years – too fast for our bodies and digestive systems to adapt. We've gone from eating wholefoods prepared using traditional methods, such as slow cooking, soaking, sprouting and fermentation, to a diet of processed foods made with refined grains and sugars, and processed seed oils.

Unfortunately, bread has been one of the biggest casualties in our industrialised way of eating, and fermented, grain-rich loaves that take up to 24 hours to prepare have largely been replaced by factory-processed versions churned out every hour.

A good-quality traditional sourdough is made with a starter culture, which has the extra benefits of lactic acids, enzymes and flavour. The starter is mixed with water and flour and left to ferment for a day, something that rarely occurs in commercial bakeries. The result is a much more digestible, delicious loaf. It lasts longer this way, too.

In terms of grains, nature has given us so many wonderful options. Some varieties of wheat, such as durum and spelt, are lower in gluten, while rice, amaranth, buckwheat and quinoa have no gluten at all. I like to mix it up by using different combinations in various recipes, but I particularly love buckwheat and spelt in baking, quinoa and barley in soups and brown rice for everything else!

HOW TO PREPARE GRAINS

It's so easy you can do it in your sleep! Just pop your grains in a bowl, cover with warm water and add a teaspoon of lemon juice, whey or natural yoghurt per ½ cup of dry grains. Cover with a tea towel and leave at room temperature overnight. The following day, drain, rinse and cook as usual – although this process usually cuts down the cooking time, which is an added bonus. If you forget to soak your grains, eating them with foods that contain fat-soluble vitamins will enhance mineral absorption – good-quality ghee, butter, cream and egg yolks are all great options.

HOW TO PREPARE LEGUMES

Legumes include chickpeas, lentils and beans, such as red kidney, cannellini and black beans. (Although peanuts are technically legumes, most people use them in a similar way to nuts or seeds.) Soak 1 cup of legumes in warm water with 1 tablespoon of whey or yoghurt or 2 teaspoons of lemon juice or vinegar. If you can get your hands on a small piece of kombu, add it to the bowl as it's a great little seaweed that helps to break down the compounds that cause flatulence. Cover with a tea towel and soak overnight. The following day, rinse, drain and cook as usual.

HOW TO PREPARE NUTS AND SEEDS

Soaking and drying nuts and seeds is known as 'activating'. To activate nuts and seeds, soak them in water with a pinch of sea salt for about 24 hours. Drain well then spread out on baking trays and dry in the oven at the lowest possible temperature (less than 50°C) for 12–24 hours or until they are very dry and crisp (or use a dehydrator). It's worth doing a big batch to make this as energy efficient as possible. It's a bit of work (and I'll be the first to admit that I rarely do this), but nuts and seeds taste *amazing* prepared this way. Simply dry-toasting them for a few minutes also helps to improve digestibility, plus they taste much more flavoursome, so this is what I usually do.

I just want to note that all of the preparation information above is 'best case scenario'. In reality, I often forget to soak grains, legumes, nuts and seeds (or I simply don't have time), but it doesn't stop me from cooking with them anyway!

BUTTERMILK DATE SCONES

MAKES ABOUT 15

Who doesn't love a good, old-fashioned scone? They were actually the first thing I ever cooked when I was around seven years old. I'd go around the neighbourhood selling them for 50 cents each and they'd fly out the door. I still bake them weekly for an afternoon treat. I particularly enjoy them with a cup of tea on the deck when Archie takes his nap. Because they're so quick and easy, they're perfect to make as a warm welcome for unexpected visitors. I've tried many recipes, and the trick to the perfect scone is in the dough. Make sure that it's soft and a little sticky, and don't overwork it as this is what leads to stodgy scones rather than soft, pillowy ones. The key is to just bring the dough together, and then pat it out (no rolling) onto a lightly floured surface. You can't call yourself a real country cook unless you can make a decent batch of scones!

300 g (2 cups) white self-raising flour, plus extra for dusting

320 g (2 cups) wholemeal self-raising flour

1 teaspoon sea salt

150 g butter, chilled and cut into 1 cm cubes

140 g (1 cup) pitted dates, chopped

500 ml (2 cups) buttermilk (for a recipe see my note on page 236)

milk, for brushing

Preheat the oven to 180°C. Line a baking tray with baking paper and dust lightly with flour.

Combine the flours and sea salt in a large bowl and stir until well combined. Add the butter to the flour and rub between your fingers until the mixture resembles coarse breadcrumbs. Stir through the dates. Make a well in the centre and pour in the buttermilk. Using one hand, mix the buttermilk into the flour with a circular motion until it just comes together as a sticky dough. The trick with scones is to not overdo this part so they stay fluffy and airy.

Lay the dough on a floured work surface and use the heel of your hand to gently press it out to a thickness of about 4 cm. Dip an 8–9 cm scone cutter in flour, press out your scones and arrange them on the baking paper. Pat together any loose ends to make extra scones or odd shapes that you can use as testers. I like my scones to look a little rough and rustic so I avoid getting the top and side too smooth. Brush the top of the scones with milk and bake for about 15–20 minutes until golden brown. The house will smell amazing!

Make a pot of tea and serve the scones warm with butter or cream and jam (such as my Strawberry and Chia Jam on page 247). The scones store well in an airtight container in the fridge for about a week.

SERVES 8–10

There's a reason why carrot cake is such a favourite – deliciousness! But this one happens to be packed with goodness without compromising on taste. It's gluten free with a guilt-free creamy ricotta icing on top.

350 g (3 cups) almond meal

2 teaspoons vanilla powder or extract, or 1 vanilla pod, split and seeds scraped

2 teaspoons ground cinnamon

½ teaspoon ground nutmeg

2 teaspoons gluten free baking powder

125 ml (½ cup) maple syrup

60 ml (¼ cup) macadamia oil

zest of ½ orange (optional)

juice of ½ orange

3 eggs, lightly beaten

500 g (about 4) carrots, grated

70 g (½ cup) pumpkin seeds, toasted

55 g (½ cup) chopped walnuts

Icing

200 g (1 cup) ricotta (for a recipe see page 86)

30 g maple syrup or honey

pinch of ground cinnamon

few drops of vanilla extract

40 g (¼ cup) almonds, toasted

25 g (¼ cup) walnuts, chopped

Preheat the oven to 180°C. Grease a 20 cm round cake tin and line the base with baking paper.

Place the almond meal, vanilla, cinnamon, nutmeg and baking powder in a bowl and mix with a wooden spoon. Add the maple syrup, oil, orange zest (if using), orange juice and eggs, and stir until combined. Gently fold in the grated carrot, followed by the pumpkin seeds and walnuts.

Pour the mixture into the cake tin, making sure you leave behind about a tablespoon to taste! It's delicious! Then bake for 1 hour or until a skewer inserted in the centre of the cake comes out clean.

Leave to rest in the tin for 15 minutes, then turn out onto a wire rack and allow to cool completely.

Meanwhile, use an electric mixer to beat together the ricotta, maple syrup or honey, cinnamon and vanilla in a bowl. Add 2 tablespoons of water and continue beating until the mixture is smooth and airy. Cover and refrigerate until needed.

When the cake has cooled, spread the ricotta frosting on top with a spatula and top with toasted almonds and walnuts. Store in the fridge for up to 3 days.

BLUEBERRY CRUMBLE BUTTERMILK MUFFINS

MAKES 12

Muffins are my weakness, especially when they come with a crumbly top, and this wholesome version is totally guilt free. There's no refined sugar, and it's filled with the goodness of barley flour, oats, seeds, nuts, buttermilk and nature's super-antioxidant fruit: blueberries. These are the muffins you want around for breakfast, afternoon tea and hectic days when there's little time for a healthy meal. Plus, they're a great addition to any lunchbox.

225 g (1½ cups) self-raising flour

70 g (½ cup) barley flour

80 g (½ cup) wholemeal flour

1 teaspoon baking powder

¼ teaspoon bicarbonate of soda

75 g (⅓ cup) rapadura sugar

375 ml (1½ cups) buttermilk
    (see note)

2 eggs, lightly beaten

60 ml (¼ cup) melted coconut oil

2 tablespoons maple syrup

1 teaspoon vanilla extract

1 teaspoon lemon zest

250 g blueberries, plus extra
    to serve

Greek yoghurt, to serve (optional)

Crumble topping

1 tablespoon barley flour

2 tablespoons rolled oats

1 tablespoon shredded coconut

2 teaspoons linseeds

pinch of ground cinnamon

30 g salted butter, softened
    (or 30 g coconut oil)

2 tablespoons roughly chopped
    pecans (or almonds or
    hazelnuts)

1 tablespoon rapadura sugar

To make the crumble topping, place the flour, oats, coconut, linseeds, cinnamon and butter in a mixing bowl. Using your fingertips, rub the butter into the dry ingredients until well combined. Stir in the pecans and sugar. Cover and refrigerate until required.

Preheat the oven to 210°C and line a 12-hole muffin tin with paper cases.

Place the flours, baking powder, bicarb soda and sugar in a bowl and stir until well combined. Make a well in the centre.

Combine the buttermilk, egg, coconut oil, maple syrup and vanilla in another bowl or jug and mix well. Pour the milk mixture into the well in the dry ingredients. Add the zest and half the blueberries. Using a large metal spoon, gently fold the ingredients together until just combined. Do not overmix or you will have tough muffins!

Spoon the mixture evenly into the muffin cases. Sprinkle over the crumble mixture and top with the remaining blueberries. Bake for 18–20 minutes or until golden. Transfer to a wire rack to cool. Serve with extra blueberries and yoghurt for a healthy breakfast or a cup of tea for an afternoon snack.

NOTE

If you would like to make homemade 'buttermilk', add 3 teaspoons of lemon juice per 250 ml (1 cup) of milk and leave at room temperature for 10 minutes to curdle.

BAKLAVA SPELT SCROLLS

MAKES 12

Hmm... How do you choose between the aroma of cinnamon scrolls baking in the oven and the sweet stickiness of baklava? You don't need to! I've combined the two in these baklava spelt scrolls. There's no yeast in these, which means no proving, so they're quicker to make yet still light and fluffy. They're particularly lovely to bake on a rainy day, so you can enjoy the delicious, sweet cinnamon smell wafting through the home. Enjoy them warm with a hot cup of tea.

160 g (1 cup) wholemeal spelt flour

150 g (1 cup) white self-raising flour, plus extra for dusting

½ teaspoon baking powder

2 tablespoons rapadura sugar

50 g chilled unsalted butter, coarsely grated

180 ml (¾ cup) chilled mineral water

70 g (½ cup) shelled pistachios, finely chopped

35 g (⅓ cup) walnuts, finely chopped

½ teaspoon ground cinnamon

Cinnamon–honey syrup

175 g (½ cup) raw honey

45 g (¼ cup) rapadura sugar

2 cinnamon sticks, broken in half

1 small orange, rind peeled into large strips, then juiced

Preheat the oven to 180°C. Line a baking tray with baking paper.

To make the cinnamon–honey syrup, place all of the ingredients in a saucepan with 375 ml (1½ cups) of water. Bring to the boil, stirring, until the honey and sugar have dissolved. Boil uncovered for 8 minutes or until the mixture thickens slightly. Remove from the heat and set aside.

Sift the flours and baking powder into a large bowl. Return any bran from the sieve to the bowl. Stir in the sugar, then add the grated butter. Using your fingertips, rub the butter into the flour until the mixture resembles coarse breadcrumbs. Add the mineral water and stir until it comes together. Knead gently in the bowl for 1 minute until smooth. Roll the dough out on a lightly floured surface to a 25 cm x 30 cm rectangle (it should be about 5 mm thick).

In a small bowl, toss together the pistachios, walnuts and cinnamon. Sprinkle the nut mixture evenly over the dough, leaving a 1-cm border around each edge. Lightly press the nut mixture into the dough with your palm. Starting from one long side, roll up the dough tightly to form a log. Use a serrated knife to trim the ends of the roll, then cut the roll into 12 even slices.

Transfer the scrolls to the prepared tray. Bake for 25 minutes or until cooked in the centre and light golden. Pour over the warm syrup mixture, carefully turning the scrolls to evenly coat on all sides. Stand for 15 minutes, turning the scrolls twice to coat in the syrup. Transfer the scrolls to serving plates and serve warm or at room temperature.

SWEET POTATO AND WATTLESEED CHOCOLATE BROWNIES

This chocolate brownie is everything it should be: gooey, fudgy and sweet, yet it won't leave you with a sugar hangover! The addition of sweet potato is a great way of incorporating more veggies into your day (and the kids won't realise!) Wattleseeds come from the native Australian Acacia tree and have a gorgeous nutty taste with a mild hint of coffee, which goes perfectly with chocolate. From school lunches to picnics, this brownie can go anywhere, but I love it still warm when the chocolate on top is all glossy and melted with a side of coconut yoghurt. It's free of gluten and refined sugar, too.

250 g sweet potato, peeled and chopped into 3 cm pieces

125 ml (½ cup) macadamia oil

35 g (¼ cup) cacao powder, plus 1 teaspoon extra for dusting

60 g (⅓ cup) rapadura sugar

4 eggs

1½ teaspoons wattleseeds

35 g (¼ cup) chopped macadamia nuts

2 tablespoons coconut flour

100 g dark chocolate (70% cacao), roughly chopped

coconut yoghurt, to serve (optional)

Place the sweet potato in a steamer over boiling water and steam for 12–15 minutes or until tender.

Preheat the oven to 160°C. Line the base and sides of a 20 cm square cake tin with baking paper.

Combine the sweet potato, oil, cacao and sugar in a large bowl, stirring well until smooth. Add the eggs one at a time, mixing well between each addition. Continue stirring until the mixture is smooth and glossy. Add 1 teaspoon of the wattleseeds, and the macadamias and coconut flour. Mix until well combined. Spoon into the prepared tin and level the surface. Scatter the chocolate evenly over the top, pressing it lightly into the surface. Bake for 20 minutes or until the edges have cooked and the centre is still moist. Allow the brownie to cool in the tin for 15 minutes. Dust the top with the extra cacao and sprinkle over the remaining wattleseeds. Cut into 16 pieces and serve warm with coconut yoghurt, if desired.

NOTES

- A delicious variation is to scatter the top of the brownie with 1 cup of either frozen raspberries or blueberries (pressing them in lightly) before baking.
- Store the brownies in a sealed container in the fridge for up to 3 days.

DETOXING THE HOME

There are certain spaces that just make us feel instantly relaxed – day spas or a bright, sunny courtyard. Perhaps it's the lighting? Or maybe an abundance of green plants, fragrances of essential oils, fresh air or calm music. Why not recreate this feeling at home, so it becomes your sanctuary? Creating a nourishing environment at home is simple, yet it has a lasting impact on our health, energy and overall happiness. It might not be possible to do everything or eliminate all chemicals, but one or two things can be enough to create a happier, cleaner and greener space, where you can come home and unwind.

HOW TO MAKE NON-TOXIC CLEANING PRODUCTS

Making the switch from toxic cleaning products to greener versions, made with all or mostly natural ingredients, goes a long way towards protecting ourselves from harmful chemicals. This is something I became particularly conscious about when I fell pregnant, and I found that it's surprisingly easy and cheap to do. Water, white vinegar, baking soda, rubbing alcohol, citrus peels or juice and essential oils like eucalyptus and tea tree are excellent basics to have on hand for cleaning.

Citrus and rosemary all-purpose cleaner

Place some citrus peels in a jar, cover with salt and leave for around 30 minutes to draw out the oils. Cover halfway with white vinegar and top up with water. Close the jar and leave it to work its magic for 2 weeks. Strain the liquid and pour into a spray bottle along with a rosemary sprig and a few drops of lemon, tea tree or eucalyptus oil, if you wish.

Simple scouring paste

Mix 4 tablespoons of baking soda with a tablespoon of water to form a paste. Use it to scrub kitchen sinks, ovens and bathroom tiles.

Lavender disinfectant

Mix 1 part distilled water with 1 part rubbing alcohol and a few drops of lavender essential oil.

CREATE A SANCTUARY

Creating a space where you feel at home and can truly relax is so important for your wellbeing. Here are my tips for turning your home into a sanctuary.

Indoor plants

There are certain spaces and homes I walk into and instantly feel great, and I've noticed that there's usually a lot of indoor plants. Not only are they beautiful but also excellent air purifiers, helping to reduce chemicals like formaldehyde in the air. Believe it or not, the air in most homes is more toxic than the air outside! For some green inspiration head to page 116.

Beeswax candles

You know how after rain the air seems fresh? Well, there's a scientific reason for it. Moving water, such as rain and waterfalls, are natural ionisers, which means they emit negative ions that attract positively-charged, floating particles like dust, pollen, odours, toxins and moulds – so they naturally purify the air. Beeswax candles do the same thing, so not only do they add serenity and calm to any space, but, just like rain, they make the air cleaner. Unlike candles made from paraffin, which is a by-product of petroleum, they're also non-toxic.

Essential oils

The transformative power of aromatherapy is well known. Specific essential oils can be used to reduce stress or promote sleep and energy. Some of my favourites are sweet orange and lemongrass for deodorising in bathrooms, lavender for rest and ylang-ylang for relaxation and positivity. It's important to use essential oils rather than fragrances to receive the therapeutic benefits.

Go barefoot

Simply leaving our shoes at the door keeps out a lot of dirt and nasty stuff like pesticides, dust, road sealant and car oil. Walking barefoot is earthing and grounding, too.

Cleaner clothing

Removing dry-cleaned clothes from the plastic bags and allowing them to air out for a couple of days helps to remove some of the solvents and chemicals.

RASPBERRY AND LEMON THYME FRIANDS

MAKES 10

I love whipping up these friands for afternoon tea, as they're a little fancier than muffins yet still very quick and easy. They've got a little more sugar than most of the sweets I make, but for these I'm willing to make an exception. Life is all about balance and enjoyment, and sometimes it takes a sweet and zesty little morsel of goodness to hit the spot.

200 g butter

50 g (⅓ cup) plain flour,
plus extra for dusting

240 g (1½ cups) icing sugar
mixture, plus extra for dusting
(see note)

150 g (1¼ cups) almond meal

6 egg whites (see note)

200 g (1½ cups) fresh or frozen
raspberries

2 teaspoons lemon thyme leaves

2 teaspoons lemon zest

2 tablespoons finely chopped
pistachios

Melt the butter in a small saucepan over medium heat and cook, swirling the pan, for 2–3 minutes or until lightly golden. Remove from the heat and set aside to cool for 10 minutes.

Preheat the oven to 200°C. Lightly grease a ½ cup-capacity friand tin with a little of the melted butter and dust with the extra flour.

Sift the flour and icing sugar mixture into a bowl. Stir in the almond meal and make a well in the centre.

Place the egg whites in a small bowl and use a fork to lightly whisk until frothy. Pour into the well in the dry ingredients along with the cooled butter, raspberries, thyme and zest. Stir until just combined. Spoon into the prepared tin, top with the pistachios and bake for 20–25 minutes, or until golden and a skewer inserted in the centre of a friand comes out clean. Remove from the oven and allow to rest in the tin for 5 minutes. Use a palette knife to loosen the edge of each friand before turning out onto a wire rack to cool. Dust with the extra icing sugar just before serving.

NOTES

- 'Icing sugar mixture' is a combination of icing sugar and tapioca flour, which is much softer than regular icing sugar.

- Store the egg yolks in the fridge to make scrambled eggs the next day.

- Friands will keep in an airtight container for 2–3 days.

BEST EVER DIY CHOCOLATE BARS

MAKES ABOUT 10

There are few things better on a rainy day than stretching out on the couch with a good movie and some chocolate. And these chocolate bars are a revelation. I can't believe how good they taste and how easy they are to make. They're perfect as a snack and also make a lovely, elegant dessert when cut into pieces and served on a platter with some fresh fruit. The great thing about making these chocolate bars yourself (apart from knowing what's in them!) is that you can add any combination and quantity of nuts and fresh or dried fruit. The three combos I've included below are heavenly – sweet, rich, decadent and chock-full of crunch and texture! Make a few bars on a rainy day, and then enjoy them long after the grey clouds have cleared. They make a beautiful gift wrapped in some foil and recycled wrapping paper.

100 g (½ cup) coconut oil
50 g (½ cup) cacao powder
45 g (¼ cup) maple syrup
1 teaspoon vanilla extract
    or powder
½ teaspoon ground cinnamon
pinch of sea salt

Mandarin and roasted
hazelnuts

6 mandarin segments
1 tablespoon mandarin zest
70 g (½ cup) roasted hazelnuts

Blueberry, rosemary and
roasted macadamia

75 g (½ cup) fresh blueberries
1 rosemary sprig, leaves
    finely chopped
70 g (½ cup) macadamia nuts,
    roasted

Goji, coconut and roasted
pumpkin seeds

60 g (½ cup) goji berries
2 tablespoons shaved coconut
2 tablespoons pumpkin seeds,
    roasted

Grease a 20 cm x 10 cm bread tin and line with baking paper.

Melt the coconut oil in a small frying pan over low heat. When just melted, pour into a bowl and whisk in the cacao until well combined and syrupy. Add the maple syrup, vanilla, cinnamon and salt and whisk again until smooth and velvety. It's worth doing this for an extra couple of minutes to ensure that everything is very well combined, as this will prevent white bits of coconut oil poking through the chocolate once it's set. (I don't really mind this marbling but it looks nicer when it's all smooth.)

Arrange your chosen fruit and nuts at the bottom of the tin, reserving a tablespoonful for the top. Pour over the chocolate, so everything is covered, then sprinkle the extra fruit and nuts on top. Place the chocolate in the fridge for at least 2 hours to set.

Once the chocolate is set, it's time to dig in. If you're not eating it all at once, cut it one slice at a time to keep the fruit and their juices intact. You won't need to worry about this if the fruit is dried (see note).

NOTES

- I've used fresh fruit for these, but they're just as good with dried fruit. Try dried figs or raisins.
- These chocolate bars need to be stored in the fridge, as coconut oil melts at room temperature.

STRAWBERRY AND CHIA JAM

MAKES ABOUT 1½ CUPS

I stumbled upon this recipe by accident while making breakfast, realising that if I put gelled chia seeds with pureed strawberries I'd probably end up with a jam and, voila, it worked! I actually love ordinary jam, but I can't resist this one because it takes just two minutes to make, there's no cooking involved and it's free of refined sugar. Plus it's packed with fibre and omega 3. It's great swirled in yoghurt or served with whipped cream. Darren's favourite supper is jam on toast with a cup of tea, so I whipped out my new creation, slathered it on buttered sourdough toast and he loved it. I told him it took me all day to make!

500 g (2 cups) strawberries, hulled and chopped
½ teaspoon vanilla extract or powder
1 tablespoon apple cider vinegar
2 tablespoons honey or maple syrup
2 tablespoons chia seeds

Place the strawberries, vanilla, vinegar and honey or maple syrup in a food processor and blitz until it forms a puree. Add the chia seeds and blitz again until well combined. Pour the mixture into a jar, seal and refrigerate for 20 minutes to allow time for the chia seeds to gel.

Your jam will keep in the fridge for 1 week, but it will probably be devoured by then! I love it drizzled over natural yoghurt and sprinkled with bee pollen, or over ricotta on toast with fresh mint leaves.

ACKNOWLEDGEMENTS

To everyone who has picked up this book, I'm beyond grateful for your support and I'm truly chuffed to share it with you.

Thank you to the dream team for making *Happy & Whole* possible. I feel so incredibly lucky to have worked with such talented, committed and beautiful people: Mary Small, Jane Winning and Lucy Heaver, thank you for believing in me and bringing my dream to life. You are all amazing, and I'm beyond grateful for your guidance, wisdom and creative genius. Rob Palmer, thank you for going the extra mile – your photography is truly exceptional. Emma Knowles, you're the best in the business – thank you for making everything more beautiful than I could have ever imagined. Big love to Daniel New for the stunning design, Sarah Mayoh and Vikki Moursellas for the food prep, my publicists Charlotte Ree and Clare Keighery, and Miriam Cannell and Helena Holmgren for your passion and attention to detail. Thanks also to Ingrid Ohlsson, Theressa Klein and Tracey Pattison, my stylist Denis Todorovic for the fashion, and Ashlea Penfold and Alexis Mahoney for the glam – you're magicians! Thank you to the bonfire shoot crew: Sophia, Max, Adam, Jasper, Lena, Carlo, Yoli and Louis. Jonathan and Maddison Pease, Vicky and Scotty, and my manager Georgie, thank you for your valuable input in my career along the way.

Thank you to the amazing Byron Bay community for your welcome, support, wisdom and generosity, for inspiring me, teaching me and changing my life. To my acupuncturist Marlene Farry, thank you for nurturing me throughout my pregnancy and beyond – you're a true healer and one of the wisest women I've ever met. Lizzie, Spell, Mel, Luciana and Lucy (Spell), you ridiculously talented and beautiful women, thank you for friendship and fashion. Also a huge thank you to Jeremy and Sarah (100 Mile Table), Adam and Lara (Punch and Daisy), Sam, Paul and Tom (Bread Social), Amanda and Andrew (Church Farm General Store), Jared Dixon (Jilly Wines), Louise (Lunch Lady), Ros and Elle (Flowers at the Farm), the whole team at The Farm, John and Lyndall (Picone Exotics), Josh and Astrid (Fleet), Palisa (Boon Luck Farm), Janelle (Byron Bay Organics), Taliah (Byron Beach Abodes), Tony (Avalon Lea), Leanne (Byron Bay Hanging Chairs), We Are Pampa, and all the passionate farmers and producers that nourish us and cultivate the best food in the world.

To my Byron mamas: Aimee, Amanda, Lena, Priscylla, Mia, Sally, Courtney, Louise, Jane and Abbie, thank you for your sageness and getting me through my first year of motherhood; team Three Blue Ducks – you're the reason we are here; my Sydney sisterhood, Jeanine, Shelly, Courtney, Ciara, Karen, Lee Bee, Libby and Kym, thank you for friendship, support, laughs, meals, wisdom and too many glasses of vino – I love you; Mike, Gemma and Berri, and Shaz and Libby, thank you for the magnificent food, funky wines and good times; my adopted Polish family, the Ofierzynskis and Kaminskis, thank you for your endless support (and incredible food!).

To Mum, Dad, Karolina, Sue, Abbie, Jamie, Thom and Sam, thanks for being the most amazing family I could hope for. Thank you for your unconditional love and for believing in me. Special thanks to Mum, there's no way I could have written this book without you. To my love Darren, thank you for your enormous faith in me and getting me to write this book, for being my biggest fan and backing me, inspiring me, challenging me and enriching my life. My baby Archie, you are my life. Thank you for the countless hours you sat on the kitchen floor playing with whisks and wooden spoons while I created, cooked and tested recipes. This book is for you. I love you both beyond measure. You make me happy and whole.

INDEX

A Plum book

First published in 2017 by Pan Macmillan Australia Pty Limited
Level 25, 1 Market Street, Sydney, NSW 2000, Australia,
Level 1, 15–19 Claremont Street, South Yarra, Victoria 3141, Australia

Design by Daniel New / UetomoNew
Editing by Miriam Cannell
Proofreading by Helena Holmgren
Index by Jo Rudd
Photography by Rob Palmer
Food and props styling by Emma Knowles
Food preparation by Sarah Mayoh and Vikki Moursellas
Colour reproduction by Splitting Image Colour Studio
Printed and bound in China by Imago Printing International Limited

A CIP catalogue record for this book is available from the National
Library of Australia.

We advise that the information contained in this book does not negate personal responsibility on the
part of the reader for their own health and safety. It is recommended that individually tailored advice
is sought from your healthcare or medical professional. The publishers and their respective employees,
agents and authors are not liable for injuries or damage occasioned to any person as a result of reading
or following the information contained in this book.

The publisher would like to thank the following for their generosity in providing locations and
props for the book: Magnolia House, Byron Bay; Avalon Lea Homestead, Byron Bay; We Are Pampa,
Batch Ceramics, Citta Design, Abode Living.

10 9 8 7 6 5 4 3 2 1